continues to drive us away from the God Who made us and the God Who loves us. The Bible is clear in giving us several ways in which we can please God. These will be presented in the last chapter of this book.

We make no apologies whatsoever for the fact that the information about God in this book is coming from the teaching of the Bible. There is no sacred writing to compete with it and nothing can replace it – it is the written revelation of God Himself controlling the human writers so that everything that was written was without error and totally reliable in every sense of that word.

May you come to believe and to know this "GOD OF THE BIBLE" and to love and serve Him all the days of your life!

Chapter 1
Does God really exist?

As I was waiting to play racquetball at a YMCA in a city where I was speaking, a young teenage girl came up to me and started telling me her life story. I stopped her after a few minutes and asked, "Why are you telling me all of this?" She answered, "I just wanted someone to talk to and you looked like you might listen!"

She was raised in a home where it was demanded that you believe in God, but there was no evidence in her parents that it made any difference. They were alcoholics and had rid themselves of her when she was just fifteen years old. She fell into the drug scene and various sexual encounters until she felt abused, lonely, bitter and suicidal. She had been arrested for drug abuse and was not put in any institution that was designed to help her.

Her real problem was the existence of God. She had a difficult time believing that there was a God Who really cared about her. She had been told that God existed and was even sent to church when she was a child. But her heart was restless and dissatisfied – the vacuum was still there, and only a personal, loving God could fill it. It was a great privilege for me that day to tell her about the God Who loves her and cares about her life and problems.

WHY DO SOME PEOPLE NOT BELIEVE THAT THERE IS A GOD?

Like that girl, some of us doubt there is a God because those who say that they believe in Him show no evidence in their lives that it makes one bit of difference. Belief in the existence of God seems to have little effect upon what some people think, say, or do. In a certain respect, they are what we might call "closet atheists." They would never admit that they do not believe in the existence of God, but their lifestyle, priorities, values and attitudes often reveal the opposite. They live as if He does not exist; they pay no attention to His presence or authority in their lives.

Our struggle with the unknown may cause us at times to deny that something exists, simply because we cannot see it or understand it. We believe in electricity, however, but we have never seen it. But, if you stick a wet finger in a socket, it might make you a believer!

One man's doubts are another man's beliefs. Experience often makes the difference. When the facts you say you believe do not bring any positive and observable results in your experience, you begin to question the validity of those facts.

SOME PEOPLE THINK THEY DON'T NEED GOD!

In a materialistic culture our "security blanket" is often found in the things that we possess. This gives us a feeling of self-worth and importance, and we relate more to the physical and material than the spiritual and unseen. In times of material prosperity, it is natural to feel that we do not need God. We are getting along fine without Him – or so we think! Moses wrote these words about 3500 years ago (Deuteronomy 8:11-14):

> *"Beware that thou forget not the LORD thy God in not keeping His*

commandments, and His judgments, His statutes, which I command thee this day: Lest when thou hast eaten and art full, and hast built goodly houses, and dwelt therein; And when thy herds and thy flocks multiply, and thy silver and thy gold is multiplied, and all that thou hast is multiplied; Then thine heart be lifted up, and thou forget the LORD thy God, which brought thee forth out of the land of Egypt, from the house of bondage."

Many people follow a materialistic viewpoint because they know that life is short and they want to enjoy it while they can. "Things" are important to them as well as the so-called "pleasures" of life. They become concerned about God when the "things" they depended upon are no longer there.

Jesus said in Luke 12:15 – *"Take heed, and beware of covetousness; for a man's life consisteth not in the abundance of the things which he possesseth."*

Many of us are blind to our own needs. We may think that we do not need God, but sooner or later we will discover differently that we do. The greater reliance upon things, the less we feel the need to depend upon God.

WHICH RELIGION IS CORRECT?

A part of the problem in knowing that God really exists is the religious confusion about this subject to which people are constantly exposed. Some religious teaching has resulted in great harm because it has often led people astray and been oblivious to the facts of the Bible. The people of Jonestown were persuaded to commit mass suicide as an honorable and God-pleasing act. Adolf Hitler used religion to manipulate the viewpoints and attitudes of people toward the Jews. In the name of religion and the honor of God many wars have been started and thousands of lives destroyed.

In an effort to discover the truth about God many people turn to religious systems with which they are more comfortable or with which they have familiarity from their backgrounds.

Some desire to seek something "new" and "different" in order to satisfy the longing of their hearts.

Muslims turn to the Koran; Mormons go to the Book of Mormon and other writings; Buddhists and Hindus have their sacred volumes to which they turn to find the existence of God and the purpose and meaning of life. Jews and Christians rely upon the Old Testament (Bible) and Christians also rely upon the New Testament. Roman Catholics add 14 Jewish apocryphal books to the Bible that Protestants accept. The number of cults and isms is staggering – which one is correct?

Many people are frustrated by the differences of opinion among the religious systems of the world and have a tendency to give up the struggle of finding the truth about God and His existence. Religious leaders want to be right, of course, and it is very hard to admit that we may be wrong. Pride stands in the way – it keeps us from pursuing the knowledge we need that others may have.

CONSIDER THE FACTS!

The facts that lead a person to believe in the existence of a personal God include:

1. The existence of the material universe
2. The order and design of the universe
3. The nature of man
4. The reliability and accuracy of the Bible
5. The Person of Jesus Christ
6. Personal experience

The Existence of the Material Universe

Two basic facts must be observed: One, that whoever or whatever made this universe was in existence before it was made! And two, whoever or whatever caused it had to have enormous power and ability.

Psalm 19:1 says: *"The heavens declare the glory of God; and the firmament* (expanse) *sheweth His handiwork."* Romans 1:20 states: *"For the invisible things of Him from the creation of the world are clearly seen, being understood by the things that are made, even His eternal power and Godhead, so that they are without excuse."*

Could the universe come into existence out of nothing? Does no one plus nothing really equal something? I have read some of the world's scientific experts on the origin of the solar system and have been astonished at two things: One, their disagreements with each other and secondly, the assumptions they must "believe" in order to make their theories possible. Are these explanations more possible and probable than the existence of a Creator Who brought it all into existence by His own power? Consider this statement by Professor Fred Hoyle, a renowned cosmologist from Cambridge University:

> *"I find myself forced to assume that the nature of the universe requires continuous creation – the perpetual bringing into being of new background material. The most obvious question to ask about continuous creation is this: Where does the created material come from? It does not come from anywhere. Material appears – it is created. At one time the various*

atoms composing the material do not exist, and at a later time they do. This may seem a very strange idea, and I agree that it is, but in science it does not matter how strange an idea may seem so long as it works."
(*Harper's* magazine, Feb., 1951, p. 68)

I find it much easier to believe in the eternal existence and power of God!

The Bible says in Hebrews 11:3: *"Through faith we understand that the worlds were framed by the word of God, so that things which are seen were not made of things which do appear."*

The Order and Design of the Universe

From the telescopic world to the microscopic world, the facts reveal amazing order and mathematical design. The laws of gravity are difficult to comprehend. Why do the planets stay in order? Who can explain the incredible processes of nature, how things grow and why things die or decay? Yes, we can study and know the laws behind these questions, but how did it all happen? Why is it that way?

In the Book of Acts in the Bible, two Christian leaders (Paul and Barnabas) confronted a pagan culture in the hills of central Turkey and said:

> *"Sirs, why do ye these things? We also are men of like passions with you, and preach unto you that ye should turn from these vanities unto the living God, which made heaven, and earth, and the sea, and all things that are therein: Who in times past suffered all nations to walk in their own ways. Nevertheless He left not Himself without witness, in that He did good, and gave us rain from heaven, and fruitful seasons, filling our hearts with food and gladness."* (Acts 14:15-17)

Nature itself is a constant witness to the presence of a superior intelligence. It speaks of plan and design, not chance or chaos.

The Nature of Man

A class in basic anatomy really makes you think! Did man just evolve from lower life forms? Is the marvel of man's physical body the result of cosmic chance? I find that hard to believe! I do not want to just sweep all the theories of evolution under the rug or become like the proverbial ostrich with my head in the sand. But, on the other hand, I have some questions that are not answered by the theories of evolution, nor is the fact of my ability to reason about these questions easily explained apart from a Creator Who has designed me like Himself – with a mind to think and an ability to reason beyond the immediate stimuli of my environment and personal needs.

In discussing my faith with a longtime friend from high school days, now teaching at one of the world's great universities in the area of physics and claiming to be an atheist, I was struck by the hopelessness of his personal views on man's existence. He is an evolutionist and believes that man is simply a higher form of animal. Realizing that his views offer little hope to the human race, he sees death as the ultimate enemy. He said, "When you're dead, you're dead!" He asked me how I could believe that man was different from the animal world. Using an old argument with me (that of comparative anatomy), he said that any school child could see that a monkey's development and bodily functions are similar to that of a human being. He argued that this gave solid evidence for the probability that we have evolved from the monkey. He added that it was only a question of time until that would be proven without a shadow of a doubt!

I said to him that with the same reasoning you could "prove" that a Cadillac evolved from a Volkswagen since they both had steering wheels, four tires, and an engine that ran on gas! Does not it rather point to a designer who knew the needs of both?

The Bible teaches that humanity (both male and female) were created *"in the image of God and after His likeness (Genesis 1:26-27)."* Man's physical body was formed by God out of the chemical elements of the soil – *"the dust of the ground (Genesis 2:7)."* Man's ability to function as a living organism was the result of the creative breath of God.

The simple beauty of the Bible's arguments about the nature of man is far more reasonable to me than the theory of evolution. The Book of Job (in the Bible) speaks very clearly concerning the evidence of a Creator:

> *"But ask now the beasts and they shall teach thee; and the fowls of the air, and they shall tell thee: or speak to the earth, and it shall teach thee: and the fishes of the sea shall declare unto thee. Who knoweth not in all these that the hand of the LORD hath wrought this? In Whose hand is the soul of every living thing, and the breath of all mankind."* (Job 12:7-10)

In Psalm 139:13-16 we read about the creation of a human being:

> *"For Thou hast possessed my reins; Thou hast covered me in my mother's womb. I will praise Thee; for I am fearfully and wonderfully made: marvelous are Thy works; and that my soul knoweth right well. My substance was not hid from Thee, when I*

*was made in secret, and curiously
wrought in the lowest parts
of the earth. Thine eyes did see my
substance, yet being unperfect;
and in Thy book all my members
were written, which in
continuance were fashioned,
when as yet there was none of
them. "*

When my wife delivered our first child
(we have three married children and
four grandchildren), I was excited with
that little baby! It was (and still is) a
marvel to me, and that great event in our
lives was another reminder of the
existence of God. There simply had to be
a Creator of enormous intelligence and
power to design such creatures as we
are. When I think of the amazing
functions of the body – the eyes, ears,
brain, nervous system, digestive system,
and so on – I cannot help but believe
that there is a God behind it all! I agree
with the Apostle Paul's words in Acts
17:28: *"For in Him we live, and move,
and have our being. "*

I Corinthians 15:39 says: *"All flesh is not
the same flesh: but there is one kind of
flesh of men, another flesh of beasts,*

another of fishes, and another of birds."
That statement is clearly a contradiction
to the theories of evolution. Humans
are unique – not simply exalted or
evolved animals!

Many people label the arguments of
those who believe that man's nature
reveals the existence of God as "blind
faith" and not based on facts. In the
book *Evolution and Christian Faith* by
Bolton Davidheiser, he writes on pages
150-151 these words:

> "...most evolutionists have faith in
> the uniformity of nature, which
> excludes miracles and other
> manifestations of supernatural
> acts of God. They have faith that
> all life on earth could have come
> about and did come about
> through the interaction of blind
> forces acting upon the kinds of
> material which were available
> before there was any life."

It is certainly "blind faith" that causes
the evolutionist to begin with nothing
and produces something as marvelous
and complex as the nature of humanity.
Surely it is far more reasonable to

believe that there exists a Creator Who made us in His own image!

Evolution must rule out the existence of God, especially a God Who created life in mature forms capable of reproduction. Evolution depends on a process which must move from species to species in its development. We are told that this process continues today, but that due to its slow development, it is not observable.

The famous "Mendel's Laws of Genetics" have shown the difficulties which the theories of evolution must face. These "laws" reveal that descent from generation to generation is orderly rather than disorderly; that variation takes place within natural species as a result of different combinations of materials already contained in the species; and that no new forms are ever created or introduced.

Moses, the great Jewish leader of 2500 years ago, claimed that God spoke to him directly and said: *"Who hath made man's mouth? Or who maketh the dumb, or deaf, or the seeing, or the blind? Have not I the LORD?"* The nature of humanity is a tremendous evidence of the presence and existence of God!

The Reliability and Accuracy of the Bible

Out of all the religious literature in our world, one book stands above all the rest in terms of authenticity, authority, reliability, and historical accuracy. Before the printing press was ever developed, the Bible was by far the most copied book in all recorded history. The thousands of copies (done by hand) reveal an amazing dedication to its preservation and respect for its uniqueness.

I told a businessman at lunch one day that I had complete confidence in the reliability of the Bible. He blurted out, "That's stupid! It's full of contradictions and fairy tales!" I asked him to tell me at least one such contradiction or myth. He could not come up with any. The truth was that he, like so many people I have met, had never read the Bible!

If I did not believe in the existence of God, I would have a difficult time explaining the unique character and message of the Bible itself. It was written by over forty different writers from different cultural backgrounds, writing over a period of 1400 years! They speak about events and circumstances outside the realm of their immediate historical context. It is an integrated "software system" as it were. They all agree about God, His plan, and His ways. These writers speak of how God spoke to them directly, telling them what to write and directing their thoughts. They predict things about the future that we now know are fulfilled and completely accurate, although much of the Bible contains prophecies that are still unfulfilled.

The science of archaeology which studies old civilizations has continued to confirm the amazing accuracy of the Bible – even when the theories of man have contradicted it for many years. The Bible speaks of great civilizations in the past that we have only recently discovered did really exist. The "digs" of archaeologists have uncovered an enormous amount of evidence as to the reliability of the Bible concerning dates, names, places, events, and people of the past.

How do you explain all of this? Is it merely coincidence? How were these writers able to predict the rise and fall of nations before they ever came into existence? How can there be so much agreement when the writers never met and lived hundreds of years apart?

The Person of Jesus Christ

How do we explain the Person of Jesus Christ without believing in the existence of God? He is without doubt the most outstanding and unique Person in the history of the world! There are over 550 prophecies in the Jewish Bible (the Old Testament) about the coming of the Messiah. These prophecies were written hundreds of years before the birth of Jesus Christ. He fulfilled many of them (over 300) by His first coming over 2000 years ago.

Who is Jesus Christ – really? His real name in Hebrew is *Yehoshua*, often abbreviated as *Yeshua*. His Hebrew name means "The LORD is salvation." The word "*Christ*" is NOT His last name!

The Greek word *(christos)* that translates the Hebrew word for "*Messiah*" *(mashiach)* was simply said into English as "*Christ.*" When Jewish people refer to Him (if they are believers in Him!) they call Him "*Yeshua HaMashiach*" – Jesus the Messiah! The word "*Messiah*" in Hebrew means "*anointed One.*"

The Bible teaches that He was born of a Jewish virgin named *Miryam* (Mary) – clearly a biological miracle. He was "conceived" according to the Bible by the power and work of the Holy Spirit. He was born in Bethlehem, Israel (a prophecy about the Messiah in Micah 5:2). After His birth, Joseph married Mary and adopted Jesus as his son. Joseph and Mary also had other children. At age twelve, his family went to Jerusalem (perhaps for his Bar Mitzvah) and Jesus astounded the great theologians and teachers of Jerusalem with His wisdom and teaching ability. His father, Joseph, was said to be a "carpenter (Greek: *teknon* – probably a stone mason)" and the family raised Jesus in the city of Nazareth in the Galilee.

At the age of 30, multitudes of people were following Him to hear His teaching and to experience miracles of healing. He healed the deaf, dumb, lame, blind, and even raised some from the dead! His ministry continued for about three years. The religious leadership of Judaism at the time had grave doubts about His claims and made plans to kill him. The Jewish leaders of the Sanhedrin charged Him with blasphemy, and then manipulated the Romans to crucify Him – even though the Roman governor, Pontius Pilate, could find no fault in Him.

According to the Bible, Jesus died on a Roman cross at the time of the Jewish Passover season, and on the "third day" after He was crucified, He arose from the dead. He was seen for 40 days after His resurrection by His disciples and over 500 people at one time! He ascended into heaven after promising His disciples that He would one day come again.

The great problem people have with Jesus is NOT His compassion and love, nor even the good that He did. The problem deals with His claims.

He claimed to be the Messiah of Israel; He claimed to forgive sins (which only God can do!); He claimed to have been sent by God the Father; He claimed to be equal with God the Father, and that He and the Father were One!

How do we explain what history and the Bible claim concerning Jesus Christ? Was He God in human flesh (as the Bible clearly teaches!) or was He simply a paranoid personality with delusions of grandeur? Was He telling the truth or was He a liar and imposter? Why did His disciples forsake Him at His crucifixion but later die for Him after His resurrection? Did the writers of the New Testament really see Him and touch Him after He arose from the dead – or is that a big lie also?

Personal Experience

A person's experience is not what we would call "objective evidence" concerning the existence of God! People can experience some incredibly ridiculous things which may or may not be a part of reality. The mind is capable of believing that something is real when it is not. What is real is often relegated to what a person "thinks" is real, but in terms of objective truth, it may or may not be real.

The experiences of those who believe in God are so varied and at times quite strange. We become very cautious about believing another person's experience, especially when trying to argue for the existence of God Himself! But, in spite of the problems and dangers involved, a person's experience is still something to be evaluated.

My parents became believers in God before I was born. I grew up in a home where it was assumed that God existed and that we were accountable to Him for our thoughts, words, and actions. As a young boy, however, there were occasional "doubts" in my mind. I knew early on that the faith of my parents had to be "real" in my own experience or I knew that one day I would deny (or at least walk away from) what they had taught me.

I began to talk to God (prayer) at an early age and wondered at times if He was there or if He was really listening to me with all the other people in the world!   I had the kind of mind that questioned many things people said and taught. I wanted facts NOT feelings! I learned to keep my "doubts" to myself so others would not pressure me to believe what they did or condemn me for questioning it.

The day that God's presence and existence became real to me was the day that I placed my faith and trust in the reliability and trustworthiness of the Bible itself. Everything I came to believe was to be found in the pages of the Bible. Either it was true or it wasn't. If it could not be trusted in some matters, how could I trust it at all!

The more I read and studied the Bible, the more convinced I became of its authority, authenticity, and power to change my attitudes and actions. I became a firm believer that God DOES exist – He is knowable and personal!

Hebrews 11:3 says: *"Through faith we understand that the worlds were framed by the word of God, so that things which are seen were not made of things which do appear."*

In Hebrews 11:6, the Bible continues: *"But without faith it is impossible to please Him; for he that cometh to God must believe that He is, and that He is a Rewarder of them that diligently seek Him."*

Romans 10:17 says: *"So then faith cometh by hearing, and hearing by the Word of God."*

That did it for me! It was my faith in the facts of the Bible itself that proved the existence of God.

Chapter 2
How Does God Speak?

If there is a God, it only makes sense to believe that He would try to communicate with the creatures He created. How does He do that? Is it possible for us to talk with Him or He with us?

As we all know, there are plenty of people around who claim that God talks to them. It gives them a feeling of superiority and dominance over others. Some of us may question them about this only to discover that we become the "enemies of God" for doubting their reliability, and as a result, they often question our own relationship to God for ever questioning them!

Does God really play favorites? Does He talk directly only to a select group (usually religious leaders!)? Does He speak audibly to anyone today? Many people claim that they have heard the voice of God! Was it loud or soft? Was He a tenor or a bass? Does He listen when we speak to Him? It is certainly easier to ask questions than to answer them!

God speaks through what He has made!

Assuming that you believe there is a God Who made the universe and all that is in it, it is then natural to expect that God would speak to us through what He has made. Consider the words of Psalm 19:1-4:

> *"The heavens declare the glory of God; and the firmament* (expanse) *sheweth His handiwork. Day unto day uttereth speech, and night unto night sheweth knowledge. There is no speech nor language, where their voice is not heard. Their line is gone out through all the earth, and their words to the end of the world."*

According to the above passage, God is constantly talking to us through His material universe – and in all languages! We learn about His *"glory,"* and His greatness. This can make you feel pretty insignificant!

Psalm 8:3-4 adds:

"When I consider Thy heavens, and the work of Thy fingers, the moon and the stars, which Thou hast ordained; What is man, that Thou art mindful of him? and the son of man, that Thou visitest him?"

A few years ago, my wife and I were flying in an airplane over the Swiss Alps. What a sight! The majestic beauty of those mountains is hard to describe to someone who has not seen them. They reminded us of the greatness of God. While straining to look out the airplane's window, I spilled my wife's coffee and was quickly reminded of the frailty of man!

If you have ever visited the giant Sequoia trees in the mountains east of Fresno, California, you have been impressed by their age and size. What trees! They speak eloquently of the greatness of the God Who made them. God's presence and greatness are revealed in the very processes of nature. Job 36:26-33 brings this truth out:

"Behold, God is great, and we know Him not; neither can the

*number of His years be searched
out. For He maketh small
the drops of water: they pour
down rain according to the vapor
thereof: which the clouds do drop
and distil upon man abundantly.
Also can any understand the
spreadings of the clouds, or the
noise of His tabernacle? Behold,
He spreadeth His light upon it,
and covereth the bottom of the
sea. For by them judgeth He the
people; he giveth meat in
abundance. With clouds He
covereth the lights; and
commandeth it not to shine
by the cloud that cometh betwixt.
The noise thereof sheweth
concerning it, the cattle also
concerning the vapor. "*

When our oldest son was just a
preschooler, he became frightened by
one of those severe Midwest storms that
sometimes hit central Ohio. When the
thunder crashed, it seemed so close (He
wasn't the only one a bit concerned
during that particular storm!). Much
damage was done. When that first great
clap of thunder hit, he asked, "Daddy,
what's that?" I said, "That's God letting

us know how great He is!" He replied, "Could you ask Him not to talk so loud?"

Psalm 148:8 says: *"Fire, and hail; snow, and vapors; stormy wind fulfilling His word."* All nature speaks of the greatness and goodness of God. We would do well to look at the flowers more often!

God speaks through supernatural acts!

The common processes of nature speak to us about God and His ways. That is true. However, God has also spoken through some unusual acts by which He has intervened in the course of human history and let us all know that He exists, is powerful, and can change things whenever He wants.

In the Bible we have the story of the children of Israel in bondage in Egypt (Exodus 5-12). Moses was chosen by God to go to Pharaoh, King of Egypt, and demand that he release the children of Israel from captivity and hard labor. Pharaoh, of course, was reluctant to believe that the God of Moses was powerful enough to pull it off or make him release them. The Bible tells us of the plagues which God performed to impress Pharaoh of His power. God said to Moses in Exodus 7:5: *"And the Egyptians shall know that I am the LORD, when I stretch forth Mine hand upon Egypt, and bring out the children of Israel from among them."*

In Deuteronomy 4:32-35 Moses reminded the children of Israel:

"For ask now of the days that are past, which were before thee, since the day that God created man upon the earth, and ask from the one side of heaven unto the other, whether there hath been any such thing as this great thing is, or hath been heard like it? Did ever people hear the voice of God speaking out of the midst of the fire, as thou hast heard, and live? Or hath God assayed to go and take Him a nation from the midst of another nation, by temptations, by signs, and by wonders, and by war, and by a mighty hand, and by a stretched out arm, and by great terrors, according to all that the LORD your God did for you in Egypt before your eyes? Unto thee it was shewed, that

thou mightest know that the LORD He is God; there is none else beside Him."

Yes, God has spoken in past history through His supernatural acts of power. In Numbers 14:11 the LORD said these words to Moses about the children of Israel in the wilderness: *"How long will this people provoke Me? And how long will it be ere they believe Me, for all the signs which I have shewed among them?"*

Those supernatural acts included bringing water out of a rock when they were thirsty and providing food (manna) from heaven and quail from the sea and guiding them with a cloud by day and a pillar of fire by night. God spoke through these miraculous signs, inviting the people to believe in Him.

In Joshua 4:23-24 we read: *"For the LORD your God dried up the waters of Jordan from before you, until ye were passed over, as the LORD your God did to the Red Sea, which He dried up from before us, until we were gone over: that all the people of the earth might know the hand of the LORD, that it is mighty:*

that ye might fear the LORD your God for ever."

The New Testament confirms this clear message: God has spoken through what He has done in the past through His miracles. I Corinthians 10:11 says: *"Now all these things happened unto them for examples: and they are written for our admonition, upon whom the ends of the world are come."*

Flavius Josephus in his monumental work on the *Wars and Antiquities of the Jews* has a brief remark about Jesus. He says that He was a *"man of miracles."* The Apostle John writes in John 20:30-31: *"And many other signs truly did Jesus in the presence of His disciples, which are not written in this book: But these are written, that ye might believe that Jesus is the Christ, the Son of God; and that believing ye might have life through His name."*

Jesus healed a man who was born blind so that he could see (John 9). When His disciples asked about the cause of his blindness and suggested that it might be the result of sin, Jesus answered: *"Neither hath this man sinned, nor his parents: but that the works of God should be made manifest in him.* " The healing of this blind man was a message from God about His power.

Many years ago I was teaching a Bible study in the home of some friends whose daughter had become very ill with a high fever. Her temperature had been between 104 and 106 degrees for about 24 hours, and since they could not get in touch with their doctor, they were becoming quite concerned.

One of the members of the Bible study was a new Christian who had never prayed publicly as yet. Upon hearing of this situation, she blurted out: "Let's pray for her right now!" I said, "That's a great idea – why don't you pray for her?" This was her first time and here is what she said: "God, if you can't heal this girl's fever right now, then I'm not going to believe in You anymore!" I was so embarrassed! I started to explain why we should not demand that God heal people because He is a sovereign God and does what He pleases. To my surprise, the fever of that little girl immediately dropped to normal and never returned! I learned a big lesson that day from one of God's miracles. They are intended to encourage us to believe in Him, and He can perform them any time He wants, even when the prayer asking Him to do it is not theologically correct! Miracles can and do exist!

God has spoken directly to certain individuals in the past!

Direct revelations of God to individuals in the past were the means by which God communicated His will and plan. The Bible records the following direct revelations in the Book of Genesis alone:

1. To Adam and Eve – Genesis 1:28-30
2. To Adam – Genesis 2:16-17; 3:9, 11, 17-19
3. To Eve – Genesis 3:13, 16
4. To Cain – Genesis 4:5-6, 9-12, 15
5. To Noah – Genesis 6:13-21; 7:1-4; 8:15-17
6. To Noah and his sons – Genesis 9:1-17
7. To Abraham – Genesis 12:1-3, 7; 13:14-17; 15:1, 4-5, 7, 9, 13-16, 18-21; 17:1-16, 19-22; 18:13-14, 17-21, 26, 28-33; 22:1-2, 16-18

8. To Abimelech – Genesis 20:3, 6-7
9. To Rebekah – Genesis 25:23
10. To Isaac – Genesis 26:2-5
11. To Jacob – Genesis 28:13-15; 32:26 -29; 35:10-13; 36:2-4
12. To Laban – Genesis 31:24, 29
13. To Joseph – Genesis 41:39

To this list, we could add the names of Moses, Aaron, Joshua, Balaam, Samuel, David, Solomon, Isaiah, Jeremiah, Ezekiel, Daniel, and many others. God spoke directly to them. Hundreds of times you will read the statement *"Thus saith the LORD,"* or *"the word of the LORD came unto me."* In II Peter 1:20-21 the Bible teaches: *"Knowing this first that no prophecy of the scripture is of any private interpretation. For the prophecy came not in old time by the will of man: but holy men of God spake as they were moved by the Holy Ghost."*

God controlled what the prophets said in terms of what was eventually written down. God guaranteed the reliability of what was written by controlling the writers with His Holy Spirit.

At the time of Jesus, God was still speaking directly, but primarily to His

Son, Jesus Christ. On one occasion when God spoke from heaven to His Son, the people who heard it misinterpreted it, thinking it was thunder or that an angel had spoken to Him (John 12:28-29).

God spoke directly to Saul of Tarsus on the road to Damascus (Acts 9:4-6) and to Ananias who helped him (Acts 9:10-11, 15-16). He spoke to Peter (Acts 10:13-16) and to Paul (Acts 18:9-10; 23:11) and to John (the Book of Revelation).

The Apostle Paul says that he received direct revelation from Jesus Christ (Galatians 1:12) and also says that the information concerning the church was revealed directly to God's "holy apostles and prophets (Ephesians 3:2-5)," who are called the "foundation" of the church (Ephesians 2:20).

God spoke directly in the past to a special group of people called prophets, but now has brought to a close those days of speaking directly to men. His final message is His Son, Jesus Christ (Hebrews 1:1-2). A clue as to the completion of God's direct messages to prophets is found in the last book of the

Bible, the Book of Revelation. In Revelation 22:18-19 we read:

"For I testify unto every man that heareth the words of the prophecy of this book, If any man shall add unto these things, God shall add unto him the plagues that are written in this book; And if any man shall take away from the words of the book of this prophecy, God shall take away his part out of the book of life, and out of the holy city, and from the things which are written in this book."

God speaks to us today through the Bible!

Though people claim that God talks to them directly, does the Bible teach that? People speak of "dreams" and "visions" and "prophecies" and declare that God has given them direct revelation. The foundation of most cults and religions is the claim of direct revelation from God. But how do we know if they are telling the truth? Does God still speak audibly and directly to people apart from the Bible?

If God truly exists and has power as the Bible describes, then we would all agree that He can speak directly to people if He wants to do it. However, we all know how easy it is for people to believe that God talks to them directly, even if the facts do not prove that He did or would. Our problem is deciding whether or not this is the way God is doing it today.

In some respects, there would be advantages to God speaking directly. It could save a lot of time and hard work. Assuming that God could speak in all the languages and dialects of the world, we would not have to go through all the trouble of learning to speak other languages and trying to translate the Bible into these languages.

The Bible was originally written in Hebrew (some portions in Ezra and Daniel are in Aramaic, the trade and court language of their time) in the Old Testament and Greek (the largest language in the history of the world) in the New Testament. Many people have a problem in hearing God speak to them through the Bible because of their language difficulties, their illiteracy, or the simple fact that they have never seen or read the Bible. If God does speak directly to people and He really cares about all language groups, then we would not need to spend so much time, effort, and money in trying to bring the Bible to them in their own language. Is God the God of the English-speaking world only? Does God not know how to speak the thousands of languages and dialects in the world?

In watching a Christian TV program recently, the speaker was claiming that God spoke directly to him. He gave some examples of things which God said to him would happen at certain times that have already proved to be incorrect. A well-known TV evangelist claims that God spoke to him directly and told him to build a certain facility, giving explicit instructions about how much money each person was to send in order to pay for it! Do you believe God did that? In my opinion, God is being blamed these days for a great deal of foolishness that is simply born in the mind of some clever and persuasive personalities!

WHAT GUIDELINES DO WE HAVE?

The Bible gives us some information as to how to evaluate people who claim that God is speaking directly to them.

1. **If it doesn't happen, then God didn't tell them it would!**

Deuteronomy 18:21-22 says: *"And if thou say in thine heart, How shall we know the word which the LORD hath not spoken? When a prophet speaketh in the name of the LORD, if the thing follow not, nor come to pass, that is the thing which the LORD hath not spoken, but the prophet hath spoken it presumptuously: thou shalt not be afraid of him."*

Religious leaders often "predict" things to establish their own authority or to persuade people to do things they want them to do. If you want people to listen, just tell them that a major event is going to happen in the near future and say that God told you to tell the world about it. If you need money, just say that the Lord revealed to you how the money should be raised. If it does not happen, you can always blame the people for their lack of faith! Just tell people that God told you they would be healed of their cancer and you will have their attention. If it fails to happen, you can always keep it quiet or accuse them of not believing enough!

The tragedy is that many people are being hurt today by all these claims of direct revelation from God. If what they say does not happen, then God never told them it would!

2. <u>If the gospel that is preached is not the gospel of Jesus Christ, then God did not speak to them!</u>

The Apostle Paul wrote in Galatians 1:6-*10* these important words:

"I marvel that ye are so soon removed from Him that called you, and would pervert the gospel of Christ. But though we, or an angel from heaven, preach any other gospel unto you than that which we have preached unto you, let him be accursed. As we said before, so say I now again, If any man preach any other gospel unto you than that ye have received, let him be accursed. For do I now persuade men, or God? Or do I seek to please men? for if I yet pleased men, I should not be the servant of Christ."

I Corinthians 15:1-11 clearly presents the true gospel of Jesus Christ. It includes the following:

(1) Christ died for our sins according to the scriptures.
(2) He was buried
(3) He rose again the third day according to the scriptures.
(4) He was seen by many people after He arose from the dead.
(5) You have to believe this gospel in order to be saved.

Other passages tell us that we are not saved by the works of the law or by our own efforts. Salvation is based on what Jesus Christ did, not what we do. Any gospel that emphasizes human merit, effort, or self-improvement is not the gospel of Jesus Christ! Any gospel that promotes health, wealth, or pleasure as the gospel of Christ is man-made, not from God! The issue is heaven or hell – where we will spend eternity! You may not believe what the Bible says, but do not be fooled by what some are saying is the true gospel.

We are warned in II John 7-11 about deceivers who do not teach the gospel of

Jesus Christ. The Bible says that we are not to receive them or even encourage them in their work.

3. <u>If what they say does not agree with the Bible, then God did not speak to them!</u>

Isaiah 8:19-20 teaches: *"And when they shall say unto you, Seek unto them that have familiar spirits, and unto wizards that peep, and that mutter: should not a people seek unto their God? for the living to the dead? To the law and to the testimony: if they speak not according to this word, it is because there is no light in them."*

A man who came to my office to tell me something very important that I needed to hear, informed me that God had directly spoken to him about a matter (included his need of financial help!). The longer he talked, the more obvious it was that his view was a direct contradiction of the Bible's teaching. When I pointed this out to him, he became indignant and started to accuse me of unbelief and of suppressing the Spirit of God Who was speaking to him – he said! I told him that it was not the

God of the Bible at all, and if someone or something did speak to him, it was probably demonic. He did not appreciate what I had to say and left my office abruptly!

4. <u>If they add any additional truth to what the Bible says, then God did not speak to them!</u>

There is no greater authority than God and the Bible! Even the church and its leaders have no authority over the Bible – they are to be submissive to what the Bible says. The Bible is a complete and final revelation from God. Revelation 22:18 says:

"For I testify unto every man that heareth the words of the prophecy of this book, If any man shall add unto these things, God shall add unto him the plagues that are written in this book."

Jude 3 speaks of *"the faith which was once and for all delivered unto the saints."* In II Timothy 3:16 the Apostle Paul wrote: *"All scripture is given by inspiration of God."*

After I finished speaking at a Bible conference where I was invited, a man came up to me to tell me the "new revelations" that God had given to him. When he finished, I asked: "What verse?" He countered, "What do you mean by that?" I answered, "Well, unless you show me where in the Bible it says what you just told me that God said to you, then I cannot accept or believe that God spoke to you." He blurted out, "This is additional to the Bible!" I said, "Then God did not tell you anything!" By the way, for your information, the "new revelation" he gave me was that God was going to blow up the world in 1975!

God speaks to us through His Son, Jesus Christ!

Hebrews 1:2 says that God has *"in these last days spoken unto us by His Son."* The Greek text literally translated says: *"In the last of these days."* What "days"? The "days" mentioned in verse 1 when God spoke directly through His prophets. In other words, God gave His final direct revelation in the Person of His Son, Jesus Christ.

The title of the last book of the Bible (Revelation 1:1) is "The Revelation of Jesus Christ." That book talks about future events and the coming of our Lord. However, the primary focus is on revealing the Person and true identity of Jesus our Messiah and King of kings and Lord of lords!

His Hebrew name is "*Yehoshua*" which means "*the LORD (Yahveh) is salvation.*" The abbreviated form of the word is simply "*Yeshua.*" In the Greek language, the word that translated the Hebrew name was "*Yesous*" which was simply said into English as "*Jesus.*"

"*Christ*" is NOT His last name! It is the English word that was transliterated from the Greek word "*christos*" which is the word used in Greek for the Hebrew word "*mashiach*" which is "*Messiah.*" The Jewish way of speaking would call our Lord "*Yeshua HaMashiach*" or "*Jesus the Messiah.*"

In John 14:8-9 Philip said to Jesus *"Shew us the Father."* Jesus answered: *"He that hath seen Me hath seen the Father."*

John 1:14 reminds us that the "*Word* (Greek: *logos* – the revelation) *became flesh and dwelt among us and we beheld His glory.*" John 1:18 says that the "*only-begotten* (meaning the unique one and only) *Son in the bosom of the Father hath declared* (displayed; revealed) *Him.*"

Yeshua, the Messiah of Israel, was born of a virgin (*Miryam* – Mary), adopted by Joseph after he and Mary were married, lived a sinless life, and died for the sins of the world, and was resurrected the third day – it was at a particular time and place in human history. He performed many miracles, healing all kinds of diseases and performing supernatural acts that only the Creator could do. He demonstrated control over the forces of nature, and claimed to forgive sin and to be able to raise the dead. He claimed that He could give eternal life to all who would believe in Him. Incredible claims! The Jewish religious leaders of His day knew exactly what He was doing and claiming. They tried to stone Him for blasphemy - their final charge that led them to manipulate the Romans to carry out the crucifixion and death of Jesus.

The "empty tomb" of *Yeshua* stands as a memorial and powerful evidence of His resurrection. If there is one fact of history that the world has tried over and over again to disprove it is the resurrection of Jesus Christ. If you wanted to destroy Christianity all you would have to do is to produce the bones of *Yeshua* and prove that He never rose from the dead!

Christianity (originally a "branch" of Judaism in that day – called "*Netzerites*" or "people of the Branch" – cf. Jeremiah 23:5-6) spread like "wildfire" among the Jewish people because of the resurrection of Jesus from the dead. It became the primary message of the apostles and it spread all over the Roman Empire to Gentiles as well as Jews.

Many people saw *Yeshua* after His resurrection. He was here teaching and preaching for 40 days before He ascended to heaven. He has promised to come again.

You may not agree with what the Bible says about Jesus Christ, but make no mistake about what it actually says. The people who lived as contemporaries of Him were not mistaken. They knew that He claimed to be God in human flesh. If He is God then God Himself has given us a revelation in human form. What better way to communicate with the human beings that He Himself had created?

WHAT ARE <u>YOU</u> GOING TO DO ABOUT JESUS CHRIST?

Nothing? Remain neutral? Impossible! You are either going to reject Him and His claims, or you are going to fall down at His feet and proclaim Him as your Lord and Savior! He is either a severe paranoid with unbelievable delusions of grandeur, or a liar and hypocrite of incredible proportions, or a victim of what others said about Him (the disciples all forsook Him at His arrest, trial, and crucifixion), or He is Who He claimed to be – the LORD of the universe, God in human flesh, our only Savior from sin, death, and hell – the choice is yours!

Chapter 3
Is God a real Person?

Depending upon something rather than a special someone does not bring real security. If God is nothing more than a force, idea, or principle, there will be little impact upon us in terms of a personal relationship or involvement. The God Who can help us the most is a personal God – One Who knows how we feel and think and Who knows our needs.

To many people, God is a security blanket. He is no more personal to them than a chair or a table. They hope He exists, but they have little knowledge of Him and no personal contact with Him. To such people, God is an "it" rather than "He." They regard God as the "force" which they hope will "be with them."

Is God like we are? Does He have a personality as we do? Does He have emotions as we have? Can we relate to Him personally as we do our friends and families? Do we share common characteristics? Does He have a body like ours? Is He physical at all? Can we see Him? Can we experience Him through the five senses?

Several years ago I asked a group of third graders what they thought God was like, and one boy said, "I hope He's like my dad." When I asked him why, he replied, "Because my dad really likes me!"

The importance of discovering that God is a real Person cannot be emphasized enough to a generation that views God from a distance and spends little time learning about Him. I believe that He is as real and personal as any one of us!

WHAT IS A PERSON?

It is very difficult to establish the personality of God without first determining what makes a person a person. One of the older viewpoints of personality is that it consists of three parts: mind, emotion, and will. But personality is more than that, since, to a certain degree, all animals reflect intelligence, feelings, and will. The Bible teaches that animals were created by God (Genesis 1:20-25), but they are

never said to be "*in the image of God*."
Only humanity is made in God's own
"image" and "*after His likeness*"
(Genesis 1:26-27).

We used to have a dog named "Angie."
She was a real lover and seemed like a
member of our family. At times, she
seemed almost human. She
communicated with us in various ways
and got very excited about seeing us
when we came home from work each
day. She obeyed our commands and
seemed to sense our moods and respond
accordingly. Although she reflected
certain characteristics of personality,
she was just a dog. Her level of
intelligence and her ability to
communicate were extremely limited.
We realize that she could neither reason
as we do nor plan for the future. She
simply responded to the direct stimuli of
her physical needs or the demands of
her environment. She could be trained
and tamed, but rational thought was
impossible for her.

A person is more than an animal,
although an animal has a physical body,
as humans do. But when man was made
"*in the image of God*" that did not refer
to a physical body, since the Bible

teaches that God did not have a physical body when man was created. Although many physical characteristics are attributed to God (such as *"the hand of the Lord"* or *"the eyes of the Lord"*), these are simply descriptions of the attributes of God in terms that we can easily understand and with which we can readily identify.

Jesus said (John 4:24) that *"God is spirit."* That means that His basic nature is spiritual rather than physical. Humans have a spirit, soul and body (I Thessalonians 5:23). Physical death occurs when the body is separated from the spirit as James 2:26 declares: *"The body without the spirit is dead."* The soul or personality of humans never dies. It is eternal, although the body will decay in the dust of the ground when physical death occurs.

The ways in which God is the same as humans deal with personality only. Humans are limited in function, ability, understanding, potential, and so on. God's personality is unlimited. Human personality has been deeply affected by sin whereas God's has not.

The Apostle Paul dealt with this problem in his message to the Epicurean and Stoic philosophers of the city of Athens. This is recorded in Acts 17:24-29. God's greatness was clearly established in that message by Paul and he clearly teaches that humans are *"His offspring."* Humanity was created by God in God's own image.

A real person exists because God exists. Personality exists because God is a Person. God did not make animals in His own image and human physical bodies are not in God's image (The physical body comes from the dust of the ground from which God made it). A human body is not the same as a person's soul and/or spirit. God is Spirit, but a human being has a spirit. A human being is not spirit alone, but spirit, soul and body.

So, what is a person? Well, let's start by saying what it is not. A person is not merely a body. A person is not an animal.

BASIC CHARACTERISTICS OF PERSONALITY

While some of these can be seen in limited ways in the animal world, it is the combination of these characteristics that makes personality what it is and the unique possession of human beings.

1. LIFE

It should be obvious that personality is a part of what lives, not what is dead. A dead body has no personality. It is said of God the Son in John 1:4: *"In Him was life; and the life was the light of men."* The Bible teaches that God *"breathed"* into man's nostrils the *"breath of life"* (Genesis 2:7) and man became *"a living soul."* John 5:26 says: *"For as the Father hath life in Himself; so hath He given to the Son to have life in Himself."*

I Timothy 1:17 states: *"Now unto the King eternal, immortal, invisible, the only wise God, be honor and glory for ever and ever. Amen."* God is *"immortal"* and *"eternal."* We live because God lives.

Deuteronomy 5:26 connects the *"living God"* with the ability to speak: *"For who is there of all flesh, that hath heard the voice of the living God speaking out of*

*the midst of the fire, as we have, and
lived?*

I Timothy 4:10 connects the *"living God"*
with salvation: *"For therefore we both
labor and suffer reproach, because we
trust in the living God, Who is the
Savior of all men, specially of those that
believe."* Because He lives, God is able
to do things which the non-living cannot
do.

Hebrews 10:30-31 says: *"For we know
Him that hath said, Vengeance
belongeth unto Me, I will recompense,
saith the Lord. And again, The Lord
shall judge His people. It is a fearful
thing to fall into the hands of the living
God."* The phrase *"the living God"* is
connected with His judgment.

In Daniel 6:26-27 the *"living God"* is
connected with His ability to deliver His
people: *"I make a decree, That in every
dominion of my kingdom men tremble
and fear before the God of Daniel: for
He is the living God, and stedfast for
ever, and His kingdom that which shall
not be destroyed, and His dominion
shall be even unto the end. He
delivereth and rescueth, and He*

worketh signs and wonders in heaven and in earth, Who hath delivered Daniel from the power of the lions. It is the God Who lives Who delivers His people. He is a real Person because He lives! The non-living is the non-personal. What comfort this should be to our hearts!

A song written by William J. Gaither says:

> *"Because He lives, I can face tomorrow; Because He lives, all fear is gone; Because I know He holds the future, and life is worth the living just because HE LIVES!"*

In Matthew 22:23-32, a group of religious teachers approach Jesus with a hypothetical problem concerning the resurrection of the dead (a doctrine which they did not believe). They said that a man died, leaving a wife without any children. The man had seven brothers who all married their brother's wife, and each one died before having any children. They then ask Jesus: *"Therefore, in the resurrection, whose wife of the seven will she be? For they all had her."* Jesus tells them that there are no marriage relationships in heaven, and knowing that they did not believe in the resurrection of the dead, He poses a problem for them to solve. He quotes Exodus 3:6 in which God said to Moses *"I am the God of thy father, the God of Abraham, the God of Isaac, and the God of Jacob"* (all of whom had died many years previous to this statement). Jesus then says: *"God is not the God of the dead, but of the living."* No Jew would deny that God is the God of Abraham, Isaac, and Jacob. But it is obvious that they were still alive at the time of Moses, even though it was over 600 years after their death!

The first and primary mark of personality is life. God is a living Person and so are we. Several years ago my wife and I were in the former Soviet Union. While in the city of Moscow, our Russian guide was quite insistent that we stand in line with thousands of Russians who were waiting to visit the tomb of Nicolai Lenin, the founder of communism and leader of the Bolshevik revolution in 1917 AD. We told our guide that we did not care to see the tomb. She asked why. I replied, "Because he is dead!" She inquired why that was such a problem. I told her that I believed in the living God and in the resurrection of the dead. We were interested in life, not death. That conversation led to three days of continual discussion (and argument!) about God and the fact that He is a Person and living. Before we left Moscow, she became a believer in the living, personal God of the Bible, about Whom she had never heard before our conversation that day in Red Square.

2. <u>SELF-CONSCIOUSNESS</u>

Some call this the fundamental mark of personality. The fact that I know that I exist, that I am aware of my existence and personality, is evidence of my personhood. One of the great statements of the Bible about the self-consciousness of God Himself is found in His words to Moses in Exodus 3:14: *"I AM THAT I AM."*

The Apostle Paul tells us in I Corinthians 2:11:
"For what man knoweth the things of a man, save the spirit of man which is in him? Even so the things of God knoweth no man, but the Spirit of God." No one knows my thoughts except God, and no man knows the thoughts of God – but

God does! God is completely and thoroughly self-conscious, whereas human self-consciousness is incomplete. That point is clearly presented in Psalm 139:23-24: *"Search me, O God, and know my heart: try me, and know my thoughts: And see if there be any wicked way in me, and lead me in the way everlasting."* Although humans have self-consciousness, we do not know ourselves as God knows us. Jeremiah 17:9-10 makes that quite clear: *"The heart is deceitful above all things, and desperately wicked: who can know it? I the LORD search the heart, I try the reins, even to give every man according to his ways, and according to the fruit of his doings."* We do not know ourselves as God knows us, but we do have a great deal of self-consciousness.

Another example of self-consciousness is the statement in John 6:6: *"And this He said to prove him: for He Himself knew what He would do."* Jesus was obviously self-conscious in this situation.

Two people can look alike physically. We call them "twins," and when there is a remarkable resemblance, we call them "identical twins." But twins can have very different personalities, and each of them is aware of his or her individuality. Each is self-conscious, and that awareness distinguishes him or her from the twin who physically looks the same. In one sense, they are the same; but in another sense, they are different from each other.

Our self-consciousness makes each of us unique and special to God. This characteristic of God's personality brings much comfort to us as it elevates us above the animal world and makes us much more than robots, fashioned just like everyone else. We are aware of our unique existence, conscious that we are unlike those around us, although we are similar in so many ways. We are special to God – made in His own image!

3. FREEDOM

Animals are not free. They cannot arise above their circumstances. Humans can, although we are not completely free as God is. Nothing outside of Himself controls the actions and decisions of God. We are free to the degree that God allows us to operate. Freedom does not mean that we can do anything we want to do, although some people teach that this is a possibility for us. Even God is not free in this sense, since God is limited by Himself. His own character and attributes control His actions and decisions. When we speak of freedom, we are speaking of the ability to determine our actions and decisions.

Daniel 4:34-37 records the words of the ancient King of Babylon – Nebuchadnezzar. After experiencing the judgment of God upon his pride for several years, he eventually had a complete change of mind and heart. He recognized the true LORD God of Israel and praised Him for the everlasting character of His kingdom. In verse 35 this king says of the LORD God of Israel: *"and all the inhabitants of earth are reputed as nothing: and He doeth according to His will in the army of heaven, and among the inhabitants of the earth: and none can stay His hand, or say unto Him, What doest Thou?"* Now that is real freedom! Job's remarks in Job 23:13 are similar: *"But He is in one mind, and who can turn Him? And what His soul desireth, even that He doeth."* Nothing outside of Himself controls God's acts and purposes. Ephesians 1:11 reminds us that God is working all things *"according to the counsel of His will."* He makes the decisions in and of Himself. He is totally free in that sense.

Psalm 115:3 says: *"But our God is in the heavens: He hath done whatsoever He hath pleased."* Psalm 135:6 adds: *"Whatsoever the LORD pleased, that did He in heaven, and in earth, in the seas, and all deep places."*

Many years ago during the days of student unrest and revolution, I was speaking about the presence and existence of God at one of our major universities. One of the students called out and said: "Can God make a rock that He cannot move?" I answered: "Yes and no. He can make a rock alright, but He will not make one He cannot move because He does nothing to violate His character. He is limited by Who He is, but absolutely free to do what He wants to do. He obviously does not want to do it!"

What about humanity? Are we free? Yes and no. We are free to do within the boundaries which God has determined and set. If we choose to sin (which, in a sense, we are free to do), we lose a measure of our freedom by experiencing the consequences of our act. Our freedom produces a loss of freedom. We are free to make decisions, but factors outside of ourselves often control our freedom. Not so with God.

I remember well the high school student who told me he was free to make his own decisions. He wanted freedom from his parents and all who were in authority over him. He started to use drugs, all in the name of freedom. His habit required more money and he started stealing. Eventually he was caught, arrested, and put in prison. When I visited him in prison, I asked: "Do you still want your freedom?" He said, "No!" His so-called freedom had now made him a slave, a captive of his own selfish and rebellious desires. Freedom to him now meant that he wanted to get out of prison where his original idea of freedom had placed him.

Some people teach that humans are not free at all. A certain fatalism characterizes their view and encourages

a passive attitude toward life, assuming
that everything is outside of their ability
to act and affect changes. That brings no
comfort at all! Our comfort resides in
the fact that being made in God's image,
we are like Him in personality. Because
He is free we also have a measure of
freedom to act, think, and speak. It is
encouraging to know that we are also
free (within certain limitations) to live
for the glory of God and not forced to act
with mindlessness and meaninglessness
in our lives.

4. <u>PURPOSE</u>

Animals have no purpose. They simply
react to the stimuli of their physical
needs or the environment. God has
purpose. Ephesians 3:11 speaks of His
"eternal purpose." His purpose
includes everything. Romans 11:36 says:
*"For of Him, and through Him, and to
Him, are all things: to Whom be glory
for ever. Amen."*

The purpose or plan of God is constantly
referred to in the Bible. Isaiah 23:9
states: *"The LORD of hosts hath
purposed it"* and Isaiah 14:26-27 says:
"This is the purpose that is purposed

upon the whole earth: and this is the hand that is stretched out upon all the nations. For the LORD of hosts hath purposed, and who shall disannul it? And His hand is stretched out, and who shall turn it back?" Isaiah 43:13 adds: *"Yea, before the day was I am He, and there is none that can deliver out of My hand: I will work, and who shall let (prevent) it?"* That is what I call a plan! Nothing can change it!

We have purpose just as God does, but our purpose is limited by His purpose and plan. His purpose includes everything; ours does not. When we react to some future goal which actually exists only in our minds, we are said to have purpose. We can react to the stimulus of future goals which have no real existence outside of our own minds. This is what we mean by purpose, and it is a mark of personality. Animals do not possess it. The difference between our purpose and God's purpose is that our purpose does not always turn out as we planned. His purpose is always fulfilled! His personality means that there is purpose to all that is happening in our lives. Romans 8:28 affirms this truth: *"And we know that all things work*

*together for good to them that love God,
to them who are the called according to
His purpose."*

A severely handicapped friend has had
much frustration over the matter of
purpose. What purpose did God have in
allowing her disability? She often asked
about the meaning of her life, being
paralyzed and confined to a wheelchair.
Because life seemed so hopeless to her
and without any design or plan, telling
her about God and His plan for our lives
has not been easy. At times, what I had
to say seemed so academic and
indifferent to her need. However, it was
the knowledge of the Bible about the
plan and purpose of God that brought
relief and joy to her. She began to
understand how the purpose of God's
personality was also a part of her. She
began to grasp the importance of
purpose in her own life and found
tremendous happiness in helping other
handicapped people. She "purposed" to
help others and "planned" what she
could do and would do. In all of this, she
discovered what being a person is all
about, in spite of a physical body that did
not function well.

My legs are a part of me, but they are not me. My hand does what I command it to do, but without its use, I am still who I am. My personality is something more than my physical body, although the two must dwell together in order for physical life to exist.

5. <u>INTELLIGENCE</u>

A certain level of intelligence exists in the animal world. They can learn to do things through training. We had to train our dog to go outside through a small door that I made in our back door. Our dog was intelligent enough to know by the sound of our voices when we were upset with her. But the intelligence of animals is limited by factors (physical needs, environment, punishment, reward, and so on) which do not limit humanity. There are three phases to the intelligence of humans which reveal the superiority they have over animals.

<u>KNOWLEDGE</u> –the perception of facts as they are. God is perfect in this regard. Humans do not always perceive the facts correctly.

<u>UNDERSTANDING</u> – the insight into the meaning of these facts. Humans have the ability to understand what animals do not possess. God has perfect understanding of all things.

<u>WISDOM</u> – the ability to relate facts to each other and use for good ends. Humans have the ability to apply what they know. God's wisdom is perfect and always good. Animals have no such ability.

I Samuel 2:3 says: *"for the LORD is a God of knowledge, and by Him actions are weighed."* His intelligence has resulted in creative acts. Proverbs 3:19-20 says: *"The LORD by wisdom hath founded the earth; by understanding hath He established the heavens. By His knowledge the depths are broken up, and the clouds drop down the dew."*

Concerning the Messiah who will come, Isaiah 11:2-3a says: *"And the Spirit of the LORD shall rest upon Him, the spirit of wisdom and understanding, the spirit of counsel and might, the spirit of knowledge and of the fear of the LORD; and shall make Him of quick understanding in the fear of the LORD."*

Three sets of characteristics that the Messiah will possess are mentioned in these verses – a total of six traits that deal with intelligence.

God's level of intelligence separates Him from humanity. God is omniscient (all-knowing) and humans are not. I John 3:20 tells us that God *"knoweth all things."* The fact that we have intelligence (a mind to think, reason, plan, etc.) results from God's placing within us His own image. We think because God thinks; We understand (though limited) because God understands. He is a personal God because He has intelligence, and that makes us real persons because we are made in His own image.

Job 28:20-28 gives us an extended look at this issue of intelligence:

"Whence then cometh wisdom? And where is the place of understanding? Seeing it is hid from the eyes of all living, and kept close from the fowls of the air. Destruction and death say, We have heard the fame thereof with our ears. God understandeth the way thereof, and He knoweth the place

thereof. For He looketh to the ends of the earth, and seeth under the whole heaven; To make the weight for the winds; and He weigheth the waters by measure. When He made a decree for the rain, and a way for the lightning of the thunder; Then did He see it, and declare it; He prepared it, yea, and searched it out. And unto man He said, Behold, the fear of the Lord, that is wisdom, and to depart from evil is understanding."

Though we know, we cannot know where the ability to know comes from – unless we look to God for that knowledge. For God is the source and Creator of intelligence in us. His ability to know, reason, and understand was given to humans when they were created in His own image (Genesis 1:26-27).

There is great comfort in knowing that God is a real Person with unlimited intelligence and understanding. We do not know why some events happen as they do, nor do we understand the purpose of many of our circumstances in life. But God knows why and we can relax in that truth! It gives us great comfort to know that God knows and understands the "why" behind every thing that happens!

6. <u>EMOTION</u>

God is emotional and has feelings just as much as we do (in fact – more!). Personality requires emotional response. Animals display what looks like emotion. They can get angry and even be sad, but their emotions in no way compare with humans. The emotions of animals are confined and limited by physical need and environment. Animals respond only to the stimuli in their immediate situation or surroundings. Humans can become emotional about the past or the future and can have feelings without facts. People can create emotional responses within the framework of their own minds. Feelings of hate and bitterness can exist when no real cause for them exists.

One woman I knew years ago is a sad example of how emotions can dominate people's lives even when there is no apparent reason for them. She imagined that people do not like her although she had no evidence that this was their actual response. When she went to the store for groceries, she believed that other people were talking about her, and even plotting to kill her. She lived in constant fear and had withdrawn herself completely from social contact with other people. The blinds in her home were always closed, although she would peek out the windows from time to time to see if anyone was outside and planning how to attack her. Fortunately, she finally went for counseling and learned to overcome her fears. Her emotions had controlled her yet they were created within her own mind. Though sad, it is another remarkable fact about personality. We have emotions that are totally unrelated to our environment or our actual circumstances.

Emotions are displayed through our physical bodies but not necessarily out of necessity. Some people feel sorrow when there are no tears, and no one can discern it by any physical characteristics. Some people love when the physical actions of the body do not show it. We are often unaware of the feelings of others, but when they are outwardly displayed, we become more aware. However, it is possible for our personality to display emotion outwardly that is not being felt inwardly. We can be deceived by outward emotional display. Hebrews 12:17 says of Esau: *"for he found no place of repentance, though he sought it carefully with tears."* The Apostle Paul wrote in II Corinthians 7:9: *"Now I rejoice, not that ye were made sorry, but that ye sorrowed to repentance."*

Perhaps no other mark of personality is as important to us as that of emotional response. We live in an age when emotions dominate. What feels good is what we determine to be right or valid for us. The word "self" has become a common word in our literature and conversations. We emphasize our needs and desires and speak often about whether anyone really cares about us. Being a real person has come to be identified with emotional response. Personality is certainly characterized by emotion and feeling but it is only a part of what personality is.

GOD IS EMOTIONAL!

God is emotional as we are – though absolutely perfect in emotional display, feeling, and concern – never deceptive or "out-of-control" or misleading. In understanding the personality of God, it is imperative that we learn of His emotional responses. We list six emotional responses for our understanding and encouragement.

God has love!

No emotion is so prominent in the personality of God than that of love. I John 4:8 tells us *"God is love."* He is not merely the emotion or principle of love, but love controls His responses and represents His essential nature and attributes.

Jeremiah 31:3 says of God's love for Israel: *"I have loved thee with an everlasting love."* His love is eternal and not affected by time or circumstances. John 3:16 says: *"For God so loved the world."* These words and countless similar verses in the Bible are most reassuring to believers that God is personal and that He deeply cares about us.

Though our ability to love is not always what we want it to be, its very presence is one of the great marks of personality. It is possible to feel love for others without ever touching them or talking to them. It is also possible to touch someone with physical affection and not feel love. Sometimes we feel physical and sexual desire by looking or touching, yet there is absolutely no regard for how the other person feels. Sexual acts can often be unloving and unsatisfactory. They may be real and powerful desires but they may reflect animal-like responses rather than true love by a personality that exists within our physical bodies. In another way of putting it, bodies function, but persons love.

Several years ago a female high school student shared with me how she had lost all respect for herself through various sexual encounters. In the course of her conversation I inquired about what she was really wanting in life. Without hesitation she said: "Someone to really love me!" She had heard from boys that she dated that they loved her only to take advantage of her sexually. She was very aware of the difference between outward appearance and the inward feelings of genuine personality. She needed to know about the love of God Himself, and that's the good news – she learned of God's forgiveness and His unfailing, unconditional, and sacrificial love for her and she became a strong believer in the Lord.

In Ephesians 2:4 we learn that God's great love is connected to His loving mercy for us, He knows what we are like but He still loves us! Mercy holds back what we really deserve!

Ephesians 5:25 urges husbands to love their wives as our Lord Yeshua loved us and gave Himself for us. The love of God is sacrificial. I John 4:9-11 makes this very clear:

"In this was manifested the love of God toward us, because that God sent His only-begotten Son into the world, that we might live through Him. Herein is love, not that we loved God, but that He loved us, and sent His Son to be the propitiation (satisfaction of God's wrath against sin) *for our sins. Beloved, if God so loved us, we ought also to love one another."*

God loved us when we did not care about Him. Romans 5:8 says: *"But God commandeth His love toward us, in that, while we were yet sinners, Christ died for us."*

Yes, God is a real Person and has emotional responses of which one of the most important is that of love.

God has hate!

While this contemporary culture that tolerates anything and everything has no desire to understand the hatred of God, it is still the clear teaching of the Bible and demonstrates His personality as it relates to emotional responses.

Psalm 5:5 says of the LORD God: *"Thou hatest all workers of iniquity."* Deuteronomy 16:22 states clearly: *"Neither shalt thou set thee up any image; which the LORD thy God hateth."* He hates the sinful actions and attitudes of the humans He created, and He hates their idolatrous practices.

Proverbs 6:16-19 says: *"These six things doth the LORD hate: yea, seven are an abomination unto Him: A proud look, a lying tongue, and hands that shed innocent blood, an heart that deviseth wicked imaginations, feet that be swift in running to mischief, a false witness that speaketh lies, and he that soweth discord among brethren."*

Isaiah 1:14 quotes the LORD when He says: *"Your new moons and your appointed feasts My soul hateth: they are a trouble unto Me; I am weary to bear them."* Worship that does not honor God is also hated by God!

A real person both loves and hates. If God did not hate, then He would not be a real Person. Hate is an emotion that troubles us all. People have often said in counseling – "I hate myself." But, the Bible argues in Ephesians 5:29 that no one has ever hated himself.

We should hate the things that people do to hurt others. We should hate injustice. And, some of us hate the telephone or the computer because of interrupting what we thought was most important or because of the problems they might create for us!

Romans 12:9 tells us that unhypocritical love will hate evil: *"Let love be without dissimulation. Abhor that which is evil; cleave to that which is good."*

God has anger!

Closely related to the emotion of hate is the emotion of anger. According to the Bible wrath or anger is a common emotion of God Himself. Romans 1:18 says *"For the wrath of God is revealed from heaven against all ungodliness and unrighteousness of men, who hold* (to hold down – "suppress") *the truth in unrighteousness."* John 3:36 states *"He that believeth on the Son hath everlasting life; and he that believeth not the Son shall not see life; but the wrath of God abideth on him."*

Revelation 14:10 speaks of the *"wrath of God"* that will be *"poured out"* upon those who worship the Antichrist instead of God Himself. Revelation 15:7 describes the final picture of God's wrath upon the earth as seven golden bowls of *"the wrath of God"* are poured out upon the earth. Revelation 16:1 calls these bowls – *"the wrath of God upon the earth."*

It is right to be angry, but it is wrong to sin in the process. Ephesians 4:26 says: *"Be ye angry, and sin not: let not the sun go down upon your wrath."* Anger in and of itself is not sinful. We ought to be angry at sin and evil. But, we are to love sinners. Anger is a real emotion that a real personality will express.

Hate and anger are closely related. Hate means that I don't like something or someone; Anger is the emotional result. My anger is sometimes displayed when the matter at hand seems very insignificant. It is easy to get angry at the failures of others. We can become angry without experiencing any justifiable reason for our reaction.

Several years ago we had a dog that was quite entertaining. She would get very angry at birds that invaded what she thought was her territory. While watching her through the window one day, I noticed that she was very upset over this one bird in our yard. She took off running after that bird. She was so excited that she slipped on the wet cement and fell right into our swimming pool! Her so-called "anger" was immediately transformed into cries for help. I pulled her out, and she played the role of a hurt puppy who needed lots of love – which, of course, she got! I'm a soft touch!

God gets angry but He never does wrong. His anger is one more piece of evidence that He is a real Person. I can relate to Him because I know what anger is like. The more I learn about God and His anger, the better able am I to understand myself and learn to control my emotional outbursts.

God has sorrow!

The Messiah is called in Isaiah 53:3: *"a Man of sorrows and acquainted with grief."* II Corinthians 7:9-11 speaks of sorrow that is *"godly."* In Jeremiah 8:18 the prophet says: *"When I would comfort myself against sorrow, my heart is faint in me."* In Genesis 6:6 we read: *"And it repented the LORD that He had made man on the earth, and it grieved Him at His heart."*

It is a mark of personality that we have sorrow and grief, and it is a great comfort to know that God feels sorrow as well. He is a real Person. He understands our tears and feels as we do about the heartaches in life. Knowing that God feels sorrow is one of the great encouragements to the believer. It helps us to relate to Him emotionally.

My sense of grief was expanded a few years ago when I experienced some deep disappointments and hurts from people whom I thought were my friends. I was astonished at their lack of concern and compassion for me in that situation. I remember feeling the hurt so deeply that I thought my insides were going to explode! I wanted someone with whom I could share my grief. I remember the comfort I received from a friend who had suffered greatly in much the same way as I had. He identified with me in so many ways that I knew he had experienced such hurt also, and somehow it helped to know that he understood what I was going through. That caused me to understand my personal relationship with God in a deeper way. God knows and feels sorrow, just as I do. He is a real Person Who can identify with what I am experiencing.

Yes, we have a Friend Who can "sympathize" with us. Hebrews 4:15 teaches: *"For we have not an high priest which cannot be touched with the feeling of our infirmities; but was in all points tempted* (tested) *like as we are, yet without sin."* Psalm 55:22 exhorts us to cast our burdens upon the Lord and He will sustain us. Psalm 62:8 says: *"Trust in Him at all times; ye people, pour out your heart before Him: God is a refuge for us."* Because God is a personal God, He can comfort us in our sorrow and grief. He Himself is acquainted with all that we feel and experience.

God has compassion!

Animals do not care, but God cares, and some people who reflect His heart will also care. Compassion is a powerful characteristic of personality that makes it unique. Psalm 103:13 says: *"Like as a father pitieth* (has compassion) *His children, so the LORD pitieth them that fear Him."*

The Bible speaks often of the mercies, graciousness, and compassion of our God. How wonderful to know! How could we doubt that He is a real Person after learning of His great compassion? Lamentations 3:22-23 states so beautifully: *"It is of the LORD's mercies that we are not consumed, because His compassions fail not. They are new every morning: great is Thy faithfulness."*

Most of us have felt compassion at one time or another – especially when we were confronted with serious human need. I felt compassion for a little five-year-old girl who was crying in the middle of one of our shopping malls because she was lost and could not find her parents. It was a joy to help her and see how her fears turned to happiness when she saw her parents again. I also felt compassion for a man without legs who was begging on the street for someone to help him get into his wheelchair. It was a pleasure to help him.

When my wife and I were in Cairo, Egypt, many years ago, we saw so much poverty in certain sections of that city that we felt compassion and pity and wished that we could do something for these people. We have often felt that way in many parts of the world where we have traveled and ministered.

Compassion is caring about people in need, and God has it in abundance because He is a real Person. His Son, our Lord Yeshua, manifested compassion on many occasions. In Matthew 9:36 we read: *"But when He saw the multitudes, He was moved with compassion on them, because they fainted, and were scattered abroad, as sheep having no shepherd."*

In Matthew 15:32 we learn again about the compassion of our Lord Yeshua: *"I have compassion on the multitude, because they continue with Me now three days, and have nothing to eat: and I will not send them away fasting, lest they faint in the way."*

One of the most beautiful stories in the Bible about the compassion of God is found in Luke 15, the story of the prodigal son. After the boy had squandered his inheritance on harlots and wound up feeding pigs, he decided to go home to his father and confess his sins. The Bible says in Luke 15:20: *"But when he was yet a great way off, his father saw him, and had compassion, and ran, and fell on his neck, and kissed him."* The father's compassion did not require that the boy crawl on his knees through the door and beg for forgiveness. The father (representing God in the story) was looking for him every day to come home, and his compassion would restore the boy back to the love and care of his father.

God has jealousy!

The strong emotion of jealousy can be rooted in bad attitudes, but it can also be based on righteous motives. Deuteronomy 5:9 describes God as a *"jealous God."* Exodus 20:5 says: *"Thou shalt not bow down thyself to them, nor serve them: for I the LORD thy God am a jealous God."* Exodus 34:14 adds: *"For thou shalt worship no other god; for the LORD, Whose Name is Jealous, is a jealous God."* Joel 2:18 speaks of the Lord's jealousy *"for His land."* Zechariah 1:14 says that the Lord is *"jealous for Jerusalem and for Zion with a great jealousy."* Zechariah 8:2 records: *"Thus saith the LORD of hosts; I was jealous for Zion with great jealousy, and I was jealous for her with great fury."*

Proverbs 6:34 speaks of how *"jealousy is a husband's fury."* Song of Solomon 8:6 says that *"jealousy (is) as cruel as the grave."* Jealousy is a powerful emotion and a very strong mark of personality. God has it, and because He feels it, there is one more evidence that He is a real Person with whom we can easily identify.

God has joy!

Personality is definitely characterized by happiness and joy. God feels joy as surely as we do. Isaiah 62:5 states: *"so shall thy God rejoice over thee."* King David wrote in Psalm 16:11: *"In Thy presence is fullness of joy."* Nehemiah 8:10 tells us that *"the joy of the LORD is our strength."* Zephaniah 3:17 says of our LORD: *"He will rejoice over thee with joy; He will rest in His love, He will joy over thee with singing."* Our God is emotional and He is a real person!

We feel joy when a new baby is born into our family. We feel joy when our children bring home a report card for which they and we parents are proud. Joy fills us when our children make the team or are chosen for special awards or honors. We have joy when our children get married and when the job we wanted becomes ours. News of a pay increase or special gifts that were unexpected can bring us joy. Joy is a common emotion in persons. And God has it also!

Yeshua told us in Luke 15:10 that *"there is joy in the presence of the angels of God over one sinner that repenteth."* Heaven is a place of joy, and God is a Person with great joy for His people!

A PERSONAL RELATIONSHIP WITH GOD IS POSSIBLE!

God is approachable and knowable. He possesses life, intelligence, self-consciousness, freedom, purpose, and emotion...and so do we! Although we are limited in the expression and depth of these characteristics, we have them because we were made *"in the image of God."* We have personalities because God does!

The Bible does not speak of God in neuter terms. He is not an "it." Personal pronouns are used of Him, and He possesses all the marks of personality. He is personal in every way, and that means that a personal relationship with Him is possible for every one of us.

Abraham was called in James 2:23 *"the friend of God."* He put his complete trust in God. Israel's King David was referred to as *"a man after God's own heart"* and in II Corinthians 6:18 we are told that God said that He would be *"a Father unto you, and ye shall be My sons and daughters, saith the Lord Almighty."* This personal relationship with the God Who made us and created us in His own image is like a family. God becomes our Father, and we become His children. John 1:12 says *"But as many as received Him, to them gave He power to become the sons of God, even to them that believe on His Name."* I John 3:1-2 declares: *"Behold, what manner of love the Father hath bestowed upon us, that we should be called the sons of God: therefore the world knoweth us not, because it knew Him not. Beloved, now are we the sons of God, and it doth not yet appear what we shall be: but we know that when He shall appear, we shall be like Him; for we shall see Him as He is."*

When we put our faith and trust in the only One Who can save us from sin, death, and hell – our blessed Lord Yeshua Who died for our sins, rose again the third day, and ascended to heaven, promising to return – we become the children of God and can experience a wonderful personal relationship with the God Who made us in His own image!

Chapter 4
Is God More Than One?

One of the most perplexing issues about the nature of God deals with the fact that more than one person is called "God" in the Bible. Christians are often accused of believing in three gods. However, the word "trinity" does not appear in the Bible, which nowhere teaches that there are three gods. There is only one God!

Christians believe that God manifests Himself in three Persons. One God, but three Persons – is that really possible?

Mathematically it is possible. Using the numeral "1" three times, we can come to two different conclusions: 1+1+1=3, but by multiplying 1 x 1 x 1 = 1. The first is a trinity, but the second a tri-unity. The word "tri-unity" is a more proper term than "trinity" when explaining the nature of God. He is three in one, or one in three respects or persons.

People have used various illustrations to reveal the essential nature of God. Some use the egg with its yolk, white, and shell. However, the yolk is not the white, and neither the yolk or the white is the shell. The illustration is inadequate. Perhaps a better one would be the chemical formula H_2O – two parts hydrogen and one part oxygen. It can appear as a gas, or a liquid, or a solid. Some believe the triangle is a better illustration. It seems upon further study that all these illustrations fall short of giving us enough adequate information on the nature of God as described in the Bible.

Sometimes we must believe when we do not fully understand. Our minds are finite, and God is infinite. We can never fully comprehend His Person or greatness. There are many things we believe yet do not understand or see with our eyes (such as electricity, wind, radio waves, and so on).

GOD IS ONE!

Here is where we must start in our understanding of Who God is. The Bible does teach that God is one, and He is the only God there is.

Deuteronomy 4:35 says: *"Unto thee it was shewed, that thou mightest know that the LORD He is God; there is none else beside Him."* Verse 39 of the same chapter states: *"Know therefore this day, and consider it in thine heart, that the LORD He is God in heaven above, and upon the earth beneath: there is none else."*

Jewish people the world over repeat what is called the "Shema" every Shabat (Sabbath Day) in their synagogues. It is based on Deuteronomy 6:4-5: *"Hear, O Israel: The LORD our God is one LORD: And thou shalt love the LORD thy God with all thine heart, and with all thy soul, and with all thy might."* Interestingly, the word *"one"* is the Hebrew word *echad* and is used in Genesis 2:24 where the man and the woman are called *"one flesh."* Two can become one in some sense – obviously. Because God is one, it does not necessarily demand that He cannot also be two or three. He is one in some sense, but can be two or three in another sense or respect.

In Isaiah 44:6 two persons are called "Yahveh" in the same verse. Here is how it reads: *"Thus saith the LORD the King of Israel, and His Redeemer the LORD of hosts; I am the first, and I am the last; and beside Me there is no God."* The first Person mentioned is *"the LORD the King of Israel."* The second Person mentioned is *"His Redeemer the LORD of hosts."* Most all commentators, both Jewish and Christian, speak of the word *"Redeemer"* as referring to the Messiah of Israel.

In Isaiah 44:8 we read in the last phrase of that verse: *"Is there a God beside Me? Yea, there is no God; I know not any."*

It is most interesting to see the phrase *"I am the first, and I am the last."* This clearly refers to the Messiah in Revelation 1:17.

Isaiah 45:5 states: *"I am the LORD, and there is none else, there is no God beside Me."* The next verse says: *"That they may know from the rising of the sun, and from the west, that there is none beside Me. I am the LORD, and there is none else."*

In Mark 12:29, Yeshua answered one of the Jewish scribes (legal experts) who asked Him about the *"first commandment of all"*: *"The first of all*

the commandments is, Hear, O Israel;
The Lord our God is one Lord."

The problem we have ~~we~~ with the unity of
God (that He is One and only One) is that
Yeshua said in John 10:30: *"I and the*
Father are one." To argue that He
meant "one in spirit" or "one in
purpose" is impossible – at least in the
minds of those who heard Him say it.
They picked up stones to stone Him for
blasphemy so they understood that He
was making Himself equal with God!

The Apostle Paul wrote about the unity
of God in I Corinthians 8:4-6: *"As*
concerning therefore the eating of those
things that are offered in sacrifice unto
idols, we know that an idol is nothing in
the world, and that there is none other
God but one. For though there be that
are called gods, whether in heaven or in
earth (as there be gods many, and lords
many), But to us there is but one God,
the Father, of Whom are all things, and
we in Him; and one Lord Jesus Christ,
by Whom are all things, and we by
Him."

The paganism of the ancient city of
Corinth is well-known. The museum

located there gives plenty of evidence of the pagan worship of a multiplicity of gods invented by the culture and leaders of the Roman/Greek world. Paul is confronting that paganism and reminding them that there is only one God!

James 2:19 says: *"Thou believest that there is one God; thou doest well: the devils also believe, and tremble."* The demons of hell are smarter than many people! They do not doubt that God is one. They know He exists and that He is the only real God there is. They tremble before Him!

Because God is one we are assured in the Bible that He has one plan of salvation that includes all who will believe it. Romans 3:29-30 makes this quite clear: *"Is He the God of the Jews only? Is He not also of the Gentiles? Yes, of the Gentiles also: Seeing it is one God, which shall justify the circumcision by faith, and uncircumcision through faith."*

There is not a separate God for Gentiles, and another one for Jews. There is only one God. There cannot be any other claim upon the human heart. That is why the Bible follows the statement of God's unity with the exhortation to love God with all of our hearts, minds, and strength (Deuteronomy 6:4-5).

The one and only God is supposedly worshiped by all religious peoples of the world. However, when we observe such worship up close, we often discover that the beliefs about this one and only God are quite diverse. God is described and understood in ways that completely contradict the views of others. When pagan cultures decide that the one and only God they worship is one among many other gods that other cultures worship, they have just denied what they say they believe. Roman society was so confused about all the ideas and concepts of God that they allowed a polytheistic view (many gods) to be the official policy of the empire.

The Bible teaches that God is one – and that there is no other god besides Him. That particular position becomes the basis for all future discussions about God. Is the Bible correct? Is its view and statements about God the only correct position on this matter? The

Bible does not allow for alternate viewpoints. We either agree or we prove it to be wrong.

BUT, IF GOD IS ONE, CAN HE BE MORE THAN ONE?

Jewish people believe (as do Christians) that God is one and there is only one God. They believe that the idea of God being more than one comes from pagan culture and Gentile influence, not from the Bible.

My wife and I lived for several years in an orthodox Jewish neighborhood. Our neighbors were dedicated to their traditions and beliefs. One day our youngest son came home and told us that his Jewish friend next door (his own age) told him that he could not play with him anymore because we were idolaters. He thought we believed in three gods, and that would make us pagans in the eyes of his family. He was told not to associate with people who believed such things. We had some explaining to do that day with our son!

The Name of God is a Plural Noun!

The Hebrew word for "God" is *Elohim*. The words *El* and *Elohe* can also mean "God." But, these last two words are singular in form, not plural. The plural form is used hundreds of times in the Bible. When referring to pagan "gods," the word is *elohim* as well. This same words is used of the one and only God. While this does not prove much, it is very interesting in its implication about the nature of God Himself. It is possible to argue that God is more than one, even though He is one in nature, essence, and being.

Plural Pronouns are Used of God!

If the word "God" referred only to a single Person, then how do we explain the plural pronouns that are used in the following passages?

Genesis 1:26 – *"Then God said, 'Let US make man in OUR image.'"*

Genesis 3:22 – *"Then the LORD God said, 'Behold, the man has become like one of US.'"*

Genesis 11:6-7 – *And the LORD said...'Come, let US go down...'"*

Isaiah 6:8 – *"Also I heard the voice of the Lord, saying: 'Whom shall I send, and who will go for <u>US</u>?'"*

To whom is God talking when He says, *"Let <u>US</u> make man in <u>OUR</u> image"*? Some say that He was talking with the angels! But if that is the meaning here, why is the phrase "to the angels" not in the text? And how do we explain Isaiah 6:8 when the Lord says *"who will go for <u>US</u>?"* He certainly was not speaking about the angels when He refers to Himself alone!

Some religious teachers believe that these plural pronouns are what they call "majestic plurals." The mean simply that God is really big! He is indeed "big" but that is not what the text teaches.

Previous to the creation of humanity, God was able to talk with Himself. If God is more than one, the use of plural pronouns is understandable.

<u>God's Name is Applied to More Than One Person in the Same Text!</u>

In Psalm 45:6-7 we read: *"Thy throne, O God, is for ever and ever; the scepter of Thy kingdom is a right scepter. Thou lovest righteousness, and hatest wickedness: therefore God, Thy God, hath anointed Thee with the oil of gladness above Thy fellows."*

The first "God" in this passage has a "scepter" and a "kingdom." This "God" also has a "God" Who has anointed Him above all others!

In Isaiah 48:12-16 we have a fascinating passage dealing with the tri-unity of God and the fact that His Name is applied to more than one Person in the same text or passage:

"Hearken unto Me, O Jacob and Israel, My called; I am He; I am the first, I also am the last. Mind hand also hath laid the foundation of the earth, and My right hand hath spanned the heavens: when I call unto them, they stand up together. All ye, assemble yourselves, and hear; which among them hath declared these things? The LORD hath loved him: he will do His pleasure on Babylon, and His arm shall be on the Chaldeans. I, even I, have spoken; yea,

*I have called him: I have brought him,
and he shall make his way prosperous.
Come ye near unto Me, hear ye this; I
have not spoken in secret from the
beginning; from the time that it was,
there am I: and now the Lord GOD, and
His Spirit, hath sent Me."*

What an incredible passage! In verse 12
the One Who is speaking says: *"I am He,
I am the first, I also am the last."* That
phrase is used of the Lord Himself in
Isaiah 41:4 and 44:6; Yet, in Isaiah
48:16, this Lord says, *"And now the Lord
GOD, and His Spirit, hath sent Me."* We
have two "Lords" in the same passage,
completely distinct from each other.

In Psalm 110:1 we read: *"The LORD said
unto my Lord, Sit Thou at my right
hand, until I make Thine enemies Thy
footstool."* In Matthew 22:41-46, Yeshua
refers to this passage in Psalm 110 and
presents the difficulty of the "son of
David" being called David's "Lord."

Yeshua said in Matthew 23:42: *"What
think ye of Christ* (Messiah)*? Whose son
is He?"* The Pharisees answered quickly:
"The son of David." Yeshua then said:
"How then doth David in spirit call him

Lord?" Then Yeshua quotes Psalm 110:1 and says, *"If David then call Him Lord, how is He his son?"* The result of this? Matthew 23:46 says: *"And no man was able to answer Him a word, neither durst any man from that day forth ask Him any more questions."* Astonishing!

The Bible presents information on the tri-unity of God if we are willing to examine the evidence without bias and prejudice. People have ways to get around these "problem texts" if one is so inclined; But, it never seems to answer the questions. It only ignores the obvious facts and seeks to interpret loosely rather than literally. The truth is, the Bible proves rather conclusively that God is more than One!

<u>Three Persons Are Each Recognized as God!</u>

In John 6:27, Yeshua said: *"Labor not for the meat which perisheth, but for that meat which endureth unto everlasting life, which the Son of man shall give unto you: for Him hath God the Father sealed."* Yeshua refers to *"God the Father."* As most religious people assume, the Father is called "God."

In the greetings of New Testament letters from the Apostle Paul, he wrote about "God our Father."

Romans 1:7 – *"peace from God our Father"*
I Corinthians 1:3 - *"Grace be unto you, and peace, from God our Father"*
II Corinthians 1:2 – *"Grace be to you and peace from God our Father"*
Galatians 1:1, 3 – *"God the Father"*
Ephesians 1:2 – *"God our Father"*
Philippians 1:2 – *"God our Father"*
Colossians 1:3 – *"We give thanks to God and the Father of our Lord Jesus Christ"*
I Thessalonians 1:1 – *"God the Father"*
II Thessalonians 1:1-2 – *"God our Father"*
I Timothy 1:2 – *"God our Father"*
II Timothy 1:2 – *"God the Father"*
Titus 1:4 – *"God the Father"*

The Apostle Peter said in I Peter 1:2: *"Elect according to the foreknowledge of God the Father."*

James 1:17 calls Him *"the Father of lights, with Whom is no variableness, neither shadow of turning."*

Jude 1:1 says *"sanctified by God the Father, and preserved in Jesus Christ."*

In the Apostle John's letters he makes it clear that the Father Who sent His Son is indeed God. In I John 4:9-10 we read of God sending His Son into the world. And, in verse 14 it reads: *"And we have seen and do testify that the Father sent the Son to be the Savior of the world."*

Yes, God is our *"heavenly Father"* and our Lord Yeshua instructed us when we pray to say *"Our Father which art in heaven."*

IS THE "SON" OF GOD THE FATHER ALSO "GOD"?

One of the most difficult teachings in the New Testament concerns the identity of the Father's Son. For example, in Hebrews 1:8 we read: *"But unto the Son He saith, Thy throne, O God, is for ever and ever."* This is a direct quotation from Psalm 45:6! Is the Father calling His Son *"O God"*? The text says it clearly. Some try to change the wording to say "God is thy throne" – making it a confessional statement by the Messiah rather than a statement about His true identity. However, that is not what the manuscript evidence of the Greek text is saying. There is one Greek text that reads that way – it is Codex Vaticanus which is the Greek text used by the Watchtower Bible of the Jehovah Witnesses, a group who argue quite strongly against the deity of the Son of God. But, the evidence is overwhelmingly against that reading.

This is not the only passage that deals with this matter of the Son being called God. Consider the wording of John 1:1:

> *"In the beginning was the Word, and the Word was with God, and the Word was God."*

In John 1:14 we read: *"And the Word was made flesh and dwelt among us and we beheld His glory, the glory as of the only begotten of the Father, full of grace and truth."*

John 1:18 continues: *"No man hath seen God at any time; the only begotten Son, which is in the bosom of the Father, He hath declared Him."*

The following facts about the opening verse of John's gospel are clear:

1. The Greek word translated "Word" is the word *logos* which primarily refers to a "revelation" of something or someone. It is the title given to the Son in this passage. He is the revelation of God.

2. The Word was *"with God"* – the preposition is the Greek word *pros* meaning "toward" or "facing" God. It requires equality.

3. John 1:1 says that *"the Word was God"* – it is clear, and there is no definite article ("the") in front of the word *"God."* (By the way, there is no indefinite article in Greek like "a" or "an"). When the definite article does not appear in front of the noun, it emphasizes the very nature and essence of the noun. This verse teaches clearly that Yeshua is God!

In John 1:14 we read: *"And the Word was made flesh."* The words *"was made"* are from the Greek verb *ginomai* which means "to become" and refers to a change of condition, not a beginning or start. The point is that the *"Word"* as the revelation of God was in existence before He became *"flesh."* He is the eternal Son of God!

But, how can the word "Son" be used of Him if He is indeed God? A good question! Yeshua is NOT a son by birth – that requires the Greek word *teknos* or *teknon* which is never used of Him. He is also NOT a child by age. The Greek word *pais* or *paidia* is not the word used when referring to the "Son of God." The word in Greek is the word *huios* which is the Greek word for "heir," the one who will receive the inheritance. Yeshua (Jesus) is the "heir of God." Consider the words of Psalm 2. In verse 2 we have the words *"His anointed"* or "His Messiah." In verses 7-8 we read these amazing words about the Messiah:

> *"I will declare the decree: the LORD hath said unto Me, Thou art My Son; this day have I begotten Thee. Ask of Me, and I shall give*

Thee the heathen (Gentiles or nations) *for Thine inheritance, and the uttermost parts of the earth for Thy possession."*

The Messiah is the Father's Son and is promised the inheritance of the nations and the earth!

Then, in verse 12 we read: *"Kiss the Son, lest He be angry; and ye perish from the way, when His wrath is kindled but a little. Blessed are all they that put their trust in Him."* What incredible words!

Romans 9:5 says: *"Whose are the fathers, and of whom as concerning the flesh Christ* (Messiah) *came, Who is over all, God blessed for ever. Amen."* The Messiah is called *"God blessed for ever"* in this verse!

In Acts 20:28 the Apostle Paul is instructing the elders of the church in Ephesus on the island of Miletus: *"Take heed therefore unto yourselves, and to all the flock, over the which the Holy Ghost hath made you overseers, to feed the church of God, which He hath purchased with His own blood."* The Father did NOT shed His blood – the Son of God did. But, this verse says that God *"hath purchased with His own blood"* – a clear identification of Yeshua as God!

There are many other references. One more may help – Isaiah 44:6 says: *"Thus saith the LORD the King of Israel, and His Redeemer the LORD of hosts; I am the first, and I am the last; and beside Me there is no God."* There are two "Lords" in this verse, and the Hebrew word for both is the tetragrammaton (four letters) referring to the sacred Name of the LORD – Yahveh! The *"Redeemer"* is clearly the Messiah in the book of Isaiah and He is identified as the *"LORD of hosts"* and as *"God."*

BUT, IS THE HOLY SPIRIT GOD AS WELL?

Some people speak of Him as the "force" or "power" as though He were an "it." Personal pronouns are used of the Holy Spirit throughout the Bible. In Acts 5 we have the interesting story of Ananias and his wife Sapphira who were both caught in a huge lie. In Acts 5:3, Peter said to Ananias: *"Why hath Satan filled thine heart to lie to the Holy Ghost, and to keep back part of the price of the land?"* But, in Acts 5:4, Peter said: *"thou hast not lied unto men, but unto God."* The Holy Spirit is God as well!

Each of the Three Persons is clearly Distinguished from the other Two!

The word *"God"* is applied to each of the three Persons but that does not make them one and the same (as some cults teach). They are separated from each other even though they are all called *"God."* In John 14;16 we read: *"And I will pray the Father, and He shall give you another Comforter, that He may abide with you for ever."* The Father Who gives the Holy Spirit is obviously separated from the Spirit in this verse. Also, Yeshua (Jesus) is also separated from the Father in that He asks the Father to give the Holy Spirit. Some cults teach that Jesus and the Father are the same Person – NOT true! They communicate with each other.

In John 14:26 we read: *"But the Comforter, which is the Holy Ghost, Whom the Father will send in My Name, He shall teach you all things, and bring*

119

all things to your remembrance, whatsoever I have said unto you." A similar thought is obvious in John 15:26 where it says: *"But when the Comforter is come, Whom I will send unto you from the Father, even the Spirit of truth, which proceedeth from the Father, He shall testify of Me."*

No matter what your theological bias, these verse are clear – the three Persons are clearly distinct from one another.

At the baptism of Yeshua by John the Baptist we read in Matthew 3:16-17: *"And Jesus, when He was baptized, went up straightway out of the water: and, lo, the heavens were opened unto Him, and He saw the Spirit of God descending like a dove, and lighting upon Him; And a voice from heaven, saying, This is My beloved Son in Whom I am well pleased."* Once again, all three Persons are separated from each other in terms of the event being described.

All Three Persons are Set Forth as One God, NOT three gods!

In John 10:30 Yeshua said *"I and My Father are one."* Some religious groups teach that this merely means "one in purpose." However, the Jews who heard that statement thought otherwise. Verse 31 says *"Then the Jews took up stones again to stone Him."* When Yeshua questioned their actions, they said that they were stoning Him *"for blasphemy, and because that Thou, being a man, makest Thyself God!"* They understood His remark as meaning that He and the Father were one in the sense that they were both God.

The Father and the Spirit are seen as one in I Corinthians 2:11 in that they know each other's thoughts: *"For what man knoweth the things of a man, save the spirit of man which is in him? Even so the things of God knoweth no man, but the Spirit of God."* The Son and the Spirit appear as one in Romans 8:9: *"But ye are not in the flesh, but in the Spirit, if so be that the Spirit of God dwell in you. Now if any man have not the Spirit of Christ* (Messiah) *he is none of His."* The Spirit of God in the believer is called the *"Spirit of Messiah."*

In John 14:16 Yeshua promises to ask the Father and He will give the Spirit to be in the believers forever. But, in verse

18, Yeshua says: *"I will not leave you comfortless: I will come to you."* In verse 16 it is the Holy Spirit Who comes, but in verse 18, it is Yeshua that comes. Then in John 14:23 we read: *"If a man love Me, he would keep My words: and My Father will love him, and WE will come unto him, and make OUR abode with him."* In verse 16, the Spirit comes, and in verse 18, Yeshua comes, but in verse 23, the Father comes with Yeshua and they make their *"abode"* in the believer. What a fantastic truth!

Why it is Necessary to Believe in the Triunity of God?

That is an excellent question and needs some thought.

1. WITHOUT THE TRI-UNITY OF GOD, IT IS DIFFICULT TO SEE HOW WE COULD HAVE A GOD OF ETERNAL LOVE!

Love demands an object to be loved. God is eternal. Before humanity was created, whom did God love? How can the eternal nature of love operate if there was no object to be loved? Some will answer: "God loved Himself."

Others say: "God loved others in His mind before they were created." That is, of course, possible; but, in terms of the object's experiencing that love, it would be impossible. If God's love demands that someone other than Himself be loved, then (prior to creation) His love is not functioning as it should. Naturally, we have entered a realm of thinking that puts a strain upon the finite mind, since it is difficult to comprehend how God's love functions now – let alone before creation!

If you believe and accept the tri-unity of God, then you have no problem. The Father loved the Son, and the Son loved the father and the Spirit, and the Spirit loved the Father and the Son!

2. WITHOUT THE TRI-UNITY OF GOD, WE HAVE NO COMPLETE REVELATION OF GOD!

Only God can reveal God completely! If Yeshua is God, then it is quite understandable to read John 1:18 and see how He put God on display: *"No man hath seen God at any time; the only begotten Son, which is in the bosom of the Father, He hath declared Him."* In

John 14:8, Philip said: *"Lord, shew us the Father, and it sufficeth us."* Yeshua replies by saying: *"Have I been so long time with you, and yet hast thou not known Me, Philip? He that hath seen Me hath seen the Father; and how sayest thou then, Shew us the Father?"* When you see Yeshua, you see the Father. God reveals God, and Yeshua is the final revelation of God!

But, how can Yeshua be called the "only-begotten Son" of God if He is really God?

The phrase *"only-begotten"* is used by the Apostle John in his writings on five occasions in referring to the Person of Yeshua HaMashiach (Jesus the Messiah). The familiar verse (John 3:16) to many folks is clear when it says: *"God so loved the world that He gave His only-begotten Son..."*

The answer to this problem is found in the grammatical meaning of the term in the Greek language. Even if a person does not know Greek, the English of Hebrews 11:17 will solve the problem. Isaac is called Abraham's *"only-begotten son."* But, Abraham had other children than Isaac (Genesis 16:15; 25:1-2). In what sense was Isaac the *"only-begotten"* son of Abraham? Hebrews 11:18 gives the answer. It was through Isaac that the promised Seed, the Messiah of Israel, would come and God would fulfill His promise to Abraham. In that sense, Isaac is the "unique" son of Abraham, not the only child ever born of Abraham. Yeshua is also the "unique" Son of God. there is no one like Him or equal to Him. Even the Greek word for *"Son"* is not the word for a child by birth or by age; it is the word for "heir." Our Lord Yeshua is the Heir of all things (read Psalm 2:1-12)!

Hebrews 1:1-3 speaks of our Lord Yeshua as the revelation of God Himself:

"God, Who at sundry times and in divers manners spake in time past unto the fathers by the prophets, hath in these last days (Literally: *"the last of these days"*) *spoken unto us by His Son, Whom He hath appointed Heir of all things, by Whom also He made the worlds; Who being the brightness of His glory, and the express image of His Person, and upholding all things by the word of His power, when He had by*

*Himself purged our sins, sat down on
the right hand of the Majesty on high."*

3. WITHOUT THE TRI-UNITY OF GOD, THERE CAN BE NO SALVATION FROM SIN!

In Mark 2:1-12, Yeshua heals a paralytic
man. In the process of healing him,
Yeshua says (v. 5): *"Son, thy sins be
forgiven thee."* The scribes who were
there said that Yeshua was blaspheming.
Their argument was centered in their
question of verse 7: *"Who can forgive
sins but God only?"* They were right, but
wrong about the true identity of Yeshua.
Only God can forgive sin. If Yeshua is
God, then He can forgive us. If He is not
God, then we have no salvation from sin
through Him. II Corinthians 5:19 says:
"God was in Christ (Messiah),
*reconciling the world unto Himself, not
imputing their trespasses unto them..."*

How important is it to believe that God is more than One?

I John 4:2-3 says: *"Hereby know ye the
Spirit of God: Every spirit that
confesseth that Jesus Christ* (Yeshua
HaMashiach) *is come in the flesh is of*

God: and every spirit that confesseth not that Jesus Christ is come in the flesh is not of God." That's very clear!

To be a genuine Christian, you must believe that Jesus Christ is God Who has come in the flesh. If Yeshua (Jesus) is not God, then He cannot save us from our sins. If He is merely man, then He is a sinner, and needs a Savior Himself! If He was only a perfect man who had never sinned, He could substitute His life for only one other person. Only God could substitute His infinite life for the sum total of all who believe in Him. The only way we can be saved is by believing that Jesus Christ is God in human flesh – the God-Man, our only Savior from sin!

Chapter 5
When was God born?

Our visit to London was thoroughly enjoyable, but our conversations with people on the streets were most perplexing. This proud British nation, once the center of the missionary movement that spread the gospel of our Lord Jesus Christ around the world, now seemed quite unaware of its roots.

One dignified gentleman who enjoyed a bit of conversation with a religious fanatic from America (his description of this writer!) was quite interested in my viewpoints about God. He reasoned: "Everything has a beginning and an end; so, when did your God begin?"

I have thought about the question a great deal since. It must seem strange to nonreligious people to believe that someone who created the heavens and the earth never had a point in time in which He Himself began to exist.

Christians, Jews, and many other religious people believe that God is eternal. He never had a beginning and He will never have an end. Is that possible? Is that consistent with the facts as we know them?

Does not everything have a beginning? I do my thinking from start to finish, from beginning to end. It is hard for me to conceive of something or someone who has always been there and never had a point of beginning. But that is exactly what the Bible teaches about God! He is eternal – no beginning or end! I know the date of my birth even though I did not have that understanding at the moment it happened. There was a time when I was not around, and my mother could remember that fact, but I don't! God has always been there.

When we talk of eternity, we usually think of it in terms of time. According to the Bible, God made time. He is above it and controlling it. One day He will get rid of time – no more watches and clocks! When I think about things, I see them in perspective to time, the sequence of events – from start to finish. I have trouble thinking about eternity and don't really understand it. I doubt if it is possible for me to comprehend it in my present frame of mind.

Several years ago, our youngest child came up to me and asked: "Dad, were you ever a baby?" Though amused at his question, I realized his problem. He had never known me as a baby and had questions about whether I was ever as small as he was. Sometimes I feel that way in relation to God. The Bible says, however, that He was never born. He has always existed. I find security in that truth, even though I don't fully understand it.

WHAT DO WE MEAN BY THE WORD "ETERNAL"!

When we speak of the "eternal" God, what do we mean? Someone who has lasted a long time? Yes, but much more than that. Our family was waiting to be seated at a local restaurant. It was crowded and we had already waited about forty minutes. My youngest son said, "Dad, they're taking forever to seat us!" In his eyes, eternity is at least forty minutes long!

When we say that God is "eternal" we basically mean two things:

1. God has no beginning or end.

2. God cannot be measured or controlled by time.

He created time itself and sees before and beyond its parameters. God is not controlled (or bothered!) by the sequence of events. He does not need a watch or a calendar!

Biblical Words that Mean "Eternal"

There are seven Hebrew words that are translated "eternal" or "forever" in the Jewish Bible, the Tanakh, or the Old Testament. There are three Greek words that are used in the New Testament. Each of these words contributes to our understanding of the eternal nature of God. Consider the following words and meanings:

<u>Old Testament Words</u>

1. NETSACH – used 34 times and means "completeness." It is used of God's anger in Psalm 103:9 and of God's presence in Psalm 16:11.

2. AD – used 48 times and means "longsuffering." It is used of God's

guidance in Psalm 48:14 and God's throne in Psalm 45:6.

3. QEDEM – used 60 times and refers to that which is "ancient" or "old." It refers to the eternal God in Deuteronomy 33:27 and Habakkuk 1:12.

4. OREC – used 93 times and speaks of "length" or that which has "no limits." It is used of the believer in God's house in Psalm 23:6 and of God's holiness in Psalm 93:5.

5. TAMID – used 103 times and refers to "continuity" or "perpetuity." It is used of God's eyes on Israel's land in Deuteronomy 11:12 and even of David's sin in Psalm 51:3.

6. DOR – used 129 times and means "dependability." It is used of God's covenant in Genesis 9:12 and of God's counsel in Psalm 33:11.

7. OLAM – used 400 times and is the basic word for "everlasting" or "unending." It refers to God's protection in Deuteronomy 33:27,

God's lovingkindness in Psalm
100:5, and of God Himself in
Genesis 21:33 and Psalm 90:2.

New Testament Words

1. AIDIOS – used twice and refers to
   that which is continuous. It
   speaks of God's power in Romans
   1:20 and the chains of darkness in
   Jude 6.

2. AIONIOS – used 6 times and
   means "unending." It is used of
   eternal life in John 3:16, God's
   covenant in Hebrews 13:20, and of
   God Himself in Romans 16:26.

3. AION – used 100 times and refers
   to an "endless period of time." It
   is used of God's Word in I Peter
   1:23 and 25, of God's throne in
   Hebrews 1:8, of God's life in
   Revelation 4:10, and of our Lord
   Yeshua in Hebrews 13:8.

The grand total of these words in terms
of usage in the Bible amounts to over
1000 times. Obviously, the word
"eternal" is a very important word in
terms of Biblical theology and

understanding. To say that God is eternal is to affect a multitude of issues, doctrines, and facts about which the Bible speaks. It affects our own understanding of the origin of all things and the control of events; it gives a unique view of history that removes doubt and uncertainty. God's eternal nature brings stability and meaning to one's life and provides wonderful assurance.

Before time began, God existed!

Genesis 1:1 (the first verse in the Bible) says: *"In the beginning God created the heaven and the earth."* The word *"beginning"* is, of course, a word of time. When things began, God was there already. He caused them to happen.

To say that God is eternal involves some important teaching about God's relationship to time. We are creatures of time, controlled by it. We cannot live yesterday nor can we live tomorrow. Today is all we have. The moment in which I just wrote that last sentence is now gone. Time implies a beginning and an end. Time is divided by God into various units of measurement, such as years, months, weeks, days, hours, minutes, and seconds. Why are there 24 hours in a day and not 30? Why not 1000 days in a year instead of the usual 365 (with a break every four years!)? Calendars have not always been the same although they were originally determined by the moon. But even then there was a fixed order, a finished design. Time was established, and it moves on, and we cannot do anything about it!

Genesis 1:14 states: *"And God said, Let there be lights in the firmament of the heaven to divide the day from the night; and let them be for signs, and for seasons, and for days, and years."* There you have it – TIME!

To say that God is eternal means that He was there before time. In Volume I of the commentary *Bereishis* (Genesis), published by Mesorah Publications of New York, we have this interesting statement on page 2 of the section entitled "An Overview – Creation":

> "Prior to creation there was nothing save the glory of God. Nothing – it is a concept that we,

creatures in a physical world, cannot even begin to comprehend, just as the blind cannot comprehend the sunset and the deaf a symphony. Can we conceive of a world without time or space? We can speak of it, think of it, but the truth is that we cannot really imagine phenomena so foreign to our experience."

Hebrews 11:3 reminds us that it is a matter of faith: *"Through faith we understand that the worlds were framed by the word of God, so that things which are seen were not made of things which do appear."* The Apostle Paul said in Romans 1:20: *"For the invisible things of Him from the creation of the world are clearly seen, being understood by the things that are made, even His eternal power and Godhead, so that they are without excuse."* Paul's point is powerful! As Psalm 19:1 says: *"The heavens declare the glory of God; and the firmament* (expanse) *sheweth His handiwork."* That fact makes us accountable. The material and physical universe reveals at least two things about God: One, that whoever made it, had to be in existence before it was made (eternal)! Secondly, that whoever made it is bigger and more powerful than we are (power)! We are accountable for those simple facts.

However, the Bible teaches that instead of building on these simple truths, humanity exchanges the truth of the Creator for something they create or make. It is the root of idolatry.

Did everything just happen? When you start to think seriously about the universe, you inevitably come up against the problem of origin. How did it all begin? The Bible makes it simple for us. It starts with the eternal God Who had no beginning or end. He is the foundation upon which everything and everyone is built. God is eternal, and that means He was there before time began!

God Exists in the Past, Present, and Future – at the same moment of time!

This point is not simply that God continues as long as time does. It is saying that the presence and existence of God encompasses all that time represents in the past, present, and future. God is not limited or controlled by it. He exists (present) in all of it (past, present, and future). Yeshua referred to this amazing truth when He said in John 8:58: *"Before Abraham was, I AM."* Those who heard Him say this immediately picked up stones to stone Him for blasphemy. They knew exactly what He was claiming. Abraham lived over 2000 years before the time that Yeshua was on earth. Yeshua did not say "before Abraham was, I WAS." That was also true. To say "I AM" is something far different from "I WAS."

Our understanding of this doctrine about the eternal nature of God (very limited – of course!) is that presently, at this very moment, God exists, and at the same time He exists at the time of Abraham, and at the same time He exists at the time of His future kingdom on earth. His presence fills it all, and His nature transcends its dimensions. We may not understand how this is possible, but we believe that this is what the Bible teaches about God.

In Revelation 4:8 the creatures (probably cherubim angels according to

Ezekiel) of heaven are praising the Lord and saying: *"Holy, holy, holy, Lord God Almighty, which was, and is, and is to come."* God has always existed and always will, and His perspective of things is not controlled by the past or the future. He sees it all in any one moment of time. That is how God was able to show the future to the Apostle John during the first century AD when he was on the isle of Patmos in the Mediterranean Sea. Many of those events that are now recorded in the Book of Revelation still lie in the future. They have not yet happened, but in God's mind and plan, they already have. John recorded the words of Yeshua in Revelation 22:13 (last chapter of the Bible) when he wrote: *"I am Alpha and Omega, the beginning and the end, the first and the last."*

One afternoon while I was enjoying a pro football game on television, one of my children became fascinated with instant replays. After a play had been completed, the television cameras would take us back in time and let us watch it over again (tough on the referees!). One of my children said: "Is that what God can do, Dad?" I asked, "Do what?" The child answered: "See the past when you're still in the present." As I listened to what that child said, I thought about the eternal nature of God. God's mind is an instant-replay machine for any past or future event!

God Dwells Outside of Time and is Not Limited by it!

Isaiah 57:15 says: *"For thus saith the high and lofty One that inhabiteth eternity, Whose Name is Holy; I dwell in the high and holy place, with him also that is of a contrite and humble spirit, to revive the spirit of the humble, and to revive the heart of the contrite ones."*

Psalm 90:4 adds: *"For a thousand years in Thy sight are but as yesterday when it is past, and as a watch in the night."* II Peter 3:8 also states: *"But, beloved, be not ignorant of this one thing, that one day is with the Lord as a thousand years, and a thousand years as one day."* God is not a victim of the clock. Time is something He invented and He controls. The Psalmist pictured the eternal God as being outside of time when he wrote in Psalm 139:16: *"Thine eyes did see my substance, yet being unperfect; and in Thy book all my members were written, which in continuance were fashioned, when as yet there was none of them."* God is on the outside, fully knowledgeable of everything time will bring. All of our days are known to Him before we experience them!

There is great freedom when you are not controlled by time or limited by it. When people say, "Take your time," it may or may not mean exactly what they said. There have been occasions when we were not aware of time. We simply enjoyed whatever time we had. God is not limited by time – He has no deadlines to meet other than what He Himself has established for us and which He Himself controls. Because He dwells outside of our time frame, He can see clearly what our tomorrows are like and what our yesterdays have been. What a marvelous perspective that gives Him!

God is the Author of Time!

Who made time? God did. Hebrews 1:2 says concerning God's Son: *"Hath in these last days spoken unto us by His Son, Whom He hath appointed Heir of all things, by Whom also He made the worlds."* In Isaiah 9:6 the Messiah is called the *"everlasting Father."* He is not the heavenly Father, but He is a *"Father"* in some sense. In reference to time, He began, designed, and controls it. That, of course, has serious implications in our lives. What happens today is not by accident or coincidence, for there is a plan that has been established by God.

Acts 17:26 refers to the fact of God being the Author of time: *"And hath made of one blood all nations of men for to dwell on all the face of the earth, and hath determined the times before appointed, and the bounds of their habitation."* God predetermined how long the nations would be in power. Their times were (and are) in God's hands! That is very comforting when you take a good long look at human history, especially the history of nations and empires.

God is Controlling Time!

Thomas Jefferson, who had such an important role in the development of

American life and beliefs in terms of government and politics, was a committed deist. In his view of God, events and circumstances are not controlled by Him. He believed that God's relationship to all things was something like winding a clock and letting it run down. God was helpless to change things and not personally involved.

The Bible, however, teaches just the opposite. God is controlling time itself and the sequence of events. That includes all the events of a person's life as Psalm 139:16 states. According to Hebrews 9:27 the day of our death is a divine appointment. In this sense, everyone dies on time, since the day when each of us will die (no matter what the means) is determined by God. The so-called "accidental death" is not really an accident at all. The means of death will vary, but when it is time, nothing will change it. The important thing is to be ready!

A little boy was sitting in front of a huge grandfather's clock waiting for it to strike twelve. He enjoyed hearing the chimes of this clock ring its twelve times, one for each hour completed. As he listened and heard, he counted "one, two, three, four....eleven, twelve" – and all of a sudden something broke in the mechanism of that clock and the chimes continued – "thirteen, fourteen..." and so on. The boy became frightened and ran to his grandmother in the kitchen and said: "Grandma, Grandma – it's later than it's ever been before!" With each passing day, we are one day closer to our death. Are we ready?

The Bible also teaches that the day and the hour of Yeshua's Second Coming has already been set by God. Yeshua said in Matthew 24:36: *"But of that day and hour knoweth no man, no, not the angels of heaven, but My Father only."* Acts 1:7 tells us that the *"times and seasons"* are in the Father's *"own power."*

One of the amazing statements concerning how God is controlling events is found in Daniel 2:21: *"And He changeth the times and the seasons; He removeth kings, and sitteth up kings; He giveth wisdom unto the wise, and knowledge to them that know understanding."* Political changes are in

144

the hands of God, whether by popular election, military coup, or royal descent. The means used is unimportant, since God is in control. All of the events of history are being operated by God Himself Who is bringing them all to a grand conclusion which He alone has designed!

We have looked at five important teachings of the Bible about the eternal nature of God:

1. Before time began, God existed.
2. God exists in the past, present, and future at the same moment of time.
3. God dwells outside of time and is not limited by it.
4. God is the Author of time.
5. God is controlling time.

That which is eternal is so because God is eternal. His Name is eternal because He is eternal. The Psalmist wrote in Psalm 135:13: *"Thy Name, O LORD, endureth for ever; and Thy memorial, O LORD, throughout all generations."*

Psalm 119:89 says: *"For ever, O LORD, Thy word is settled in heaven."* Again, in

Psalm 119:152 we read: *"Concerning Thy testimonies, I have known of old that Thou hast founded them for ever."* And in Psalm 119:160 it says: *"Thy word is true from the beginning: and every one of Thy righteous judgments endureth for ever."* God's Word is eternal because God is eternal! Isaiah 40:8 states the same thing: *"The grass withereth, the flower fadeth; but the word of our God shall stand for ever."* In addition to His word, many things will endure forever, such as His covenant, throne, kingdom, and purposes. All because God is eternal!

The everlasting God manifests many attributes and characteristics which are said to be eternal. His righteousness, power, ways, love, and salvation are all said to be eternal. Psalm 103:17 says: *"But the mercy of the LORD is from everlasting to everlasting upon them that fear Him, and His righteousness unto children's children."*

What Difference Does it Make?

Is it important to believe that God had no beginning or end? Does His eternal nature affect us in any way? If you don't

146

believe in God, what possible difference would it make?

If you are not a believer in the God of the Bible and in His Son, the Messiah of Israel, our Lord Yeshua – the eternal nature of God can be indeed frightening. The Bible teaches that a person has no excuse before God if you ignore the truth of His eternal power in the material universe which He has created (Romans 1:20). Creation does not reveal everything about God, but one thing should be obvious: Whoever made it had to exist before it was made and, therefore, must be eternal!

The most serious fact facing a person who does not believe in the God of the Bible is that the consequences of not believing in His Son, our Lord Yeshua, are eternal, not temporary. Matthew 25:46 speaks of *"everlasting* (Greek: *aionion*) *punishment."* In this verse, the same adjective (*aionion)* is used for the words *"eternal life."* Many people like to believe that the only punishment they will experience is the trouble they will have in this life. But, the Bible clearly teaches otherwise. God's punishment of the non-believer will last forever!

II Thessalonians 1:7-9 speaks of the day when our Lord will judge those who do not obey the gospel. It says that they will be *"punished with everlasting (aionion) destruction from the presence of the Lord and from the glory of His power."* Revelation 20:10 states that the devil, the beast (coming world political leader – Antichrist), and the false prophet (coming world religious leader) will be cast into the *"lake of fire"* and that their torment will last forever. In Revelation 20:15 we read that *"whoever was not found written in the Book of Life was cast into the lake of fire."* Yes, the consequences of rejecting God's Son, the Messiah of Israel, our Lord Yeshua (Jesus) are everlasting! Because God is eternal and His plan is eternal, so are the consequences upon non-believers eternal.

To the Believer – with Love!

Because God is eternal, those who believe in His eternal Son, Yeshua HaMashiach (Jesus the Messiah) as our only Savior from sin, death, and hell – will live forever! Yeshua says in John 5:24: *"Verily, verily, I say unto you, He that heareth My word, and believeth on*

Him that sent Me, hath everlasting life, and shall not come into condemnation; but is passed from death unto life."
Eternal life is the present possession of every genuine believer in Yeshua. It is not simply something you are going to receive in the future. You have it right now if you believe in Him! Notice this wonderful passage of assurance in I John 5:11-13:

"And this is the record, that God hath given to us eternal life, and this life is in His Son. He that hath the Son hath life; And he that hath not the Son of God hath not life. These things have I written unto you that believe on the Name of the Son of God; that ye may know that ye have eternal life, and that ye may believe on the Name of the Son of God."

Because God is eternal, we can count on Him to do what He has said. Psalm 105:8 states that He has remembered *"His covenant forever."* The eternal nature of God makes His counsel completely trustworthy and far superior to any reasoning and opinions of men. Psalm 33:11 reminds us that His counsel *"stands forever."* His counsel will guide us through all the difficult experiences of our lives. Psalm 48:14 says: *"For this God is our God for ever and ever: He will be our Guide even unto death."* Deuteronomy 33:27 says: *"The eternal God is thy Refuge, and underneath are the everlasting arms..."*

In speaking of God's keeping power over His people Israel, we read these wonderful words in Psalm 89:36-37: *"His seed shall endure for ever, and His throne as the sun before me. It shall be established for ever as the moon, and as a faithful witness in heaven."* Psalm 90:1 read: *"LORD, Thou hast been our dwelling place in all generations."* Psalm 91:9-10 says: *"Because thou hast made the LORD, which is my Refuge, even the most High, thy Habitation; There shall no evil befall thee, neither shall any plague come nigh thy dwelling."* What wonderful promises! God's protection and security are mentioned many times in the Bible. He will take care of His own. We have no need to be afraid – for He is the eternal God!

One of the great passages on the eternal nature of God is Isaiah 40:28-31:

"Hast thou not known? Hast thou not heard, that the everlasting God, the LORD, the Creator of the ends of the earth, fainteth not, neither is weary? There is no searching of His understanding. He giveth power to the faint; and to them that have no might He increaseth strength. Even the youths shall faint and be weary, and the young men shall utterly fall: But they that wait upon the LORD shall renew their strength; they shall mount up with wings as eagles; they shall run, and not be weary; and they shall walk, and not faint."

Though we get tired and weary, the everlasting God does not! Our protection, security, trust, and dependency is resting upon the eternal nature of our God. Because He is eternal, He is trustworthy and reliable – we can always depend upon Him!

God is controlling time and is above time. He was there before the earth was formed. As He had no beginning, so He will have no end. No start or finish, no beginning or end – simply the God Who is always there and always will be!

Chapter 6
Where is God?

Imagine for a moment that the first 40 years of your life included the best education money could buy, access to all the wealth you could ever want, and the potential of being the most powerful person on earth, ruling the greatest nation of your time. Sound good? Next imagine that through one act of violence you were forced to leave all of those advantages and spend the next 40 years of your life taking care of sheep in the desert!

Now suppose that while you were out taking care of the sheep one day, you saw a desert bush on fire, although the bush did not seem to burn. Then imagine hearing a majestic voice, speaking from the burning bush and asking you to go back to the place where you grew up (the most powerful nation on the earth at the time) and demand that the leaders release some three million people that were working as slaves for that nation. You would probably begin doing exactly what Moses did over 3000 years ago – start making excuses for why you cannot do that!

In that amazing moment of history when Moses needed some reassurance of how he could possibly do what was being asked of him, he heard these words recorded in Exodus 3:12: *"Certainly I will be with thee."* God's presence was promised.

There are times in all of our lives when the only thing that brings us comfort is the fact that God is there. To know that He really exists, and that He is present with you, will take you through some tough times and difficult trials.

In the summer of 1964 I was scuba diving in beautiful Schroon Lake, New York. The tank of air on my back had no gauge, but I was assured that it was full of air. Unfortunately, it was not! About 20 feet below the surface of the water and about 100 yards from shore, my air supply ran out – it was a case of instant panic! To this day I am not sure how I was rescued, but I woke up on the shore with a crowd of people staring at me on the ground. What I do remember was my response to God when I became aware of the fact that my air supply was gone. I said, "God, if You are there, I could sure use Your help right now!" Several verses ran through my mind during the pressure of that moment, such as: *"I will never leave you nor forsake you (Hebrews 13:5)."* Also, Matthew 28:20 which says: *"Lo, I am with you always, even to the end of the age."* I was hoping that this verse did not mean the end of my earthly existence!

What amazed me was the peace and comfort that came over me in that situation. I knew that God was there, taking care of me. There was nothing to worry about since I had made my peace with God many years before that event. I was ready to die and to be in heaven with my Lord. As it turned out, I am still around. God's presence not only comforted me in a difficult situation, but it gave me a confidence that everything would be all right.

It is difficult to answer the question "Where is God?" We cannot see God with our physical eyesight. I Timothy 1:17 refers to Him as the *"invisible God."* To ask the question "Where is God?" is similar to asking "Where is the universe?"

We have learned that God is a real Person Who exists through all eternity. He has never had a beginning nor will He have an end. But where is He? Can we locate Him? Is there a place where He can be found? The Bible admonishes us quite frequently to seek for Him, but where do we start looking?

In theological terms, we are talking about the omnipresence of God, the fact that He is everywhere. You cannot run away from Him, nor hide from His presence. Psalm 139:7-10 puts it like this:

> *"Whither shall I go from Thy Spirit? Or whither shall I flee from Thy presence? If I ascend up into heaven, Thou art there; if I make my bed in hell, behold, Thou art there. If I take the wings of the morning, and dwell in the uttermost parts of the sea; Even there shall Thy hand lead me, and Thy right hand shall hold me."*

The Psalmist asks "Where?" and the answer comes, "you are there." It is not merely the thought of God that is "there," nor is it simply His influence, as some might conclude. He is a real Person, and HE IS THERE! This is the mystery of all mysteries – the presence and existence of God. How can He be everywhere at once and still be a real Person as we are? Our finite minds are controlled by a three-dimensional world (which the presence of God permeates!) that limits our ability to conceive of things apart from bodies, buildings, places, objects, and so on.

A DEFINITION OF OMNIPRESENCE

Because we are limited by our human bodies and the ability of our finite minds, it is difficult for us to comprehend how someone could be everywhere at once. There are three essential parts of the definition of God's omnipresence, each of them equally important to our understanding.

1. God is in the universe, everywhere present at the same time!

Job 22:12 states: *"Is not God in the height of heaven? And behold the height of the stars, how high they are!"* The text argues that God is present in the place of the highest stars!

One of the best examples of God's presence being everywhere at the same time is found in Isaiah 57:15: *"For thus saith the high and lofty One that inhabiteth eternity, Whose Name is Holy; I dwell in the high and holy place, with him also that is of a contrite and humble spirit, to revive the spirit of the humble, and to revive the heart of the contrite ones."*

God says that He dwells in the *"high and holy place."* But, He also dwells with *"a contrite and humble spirit."* Several years ago there was a very popular Christian song entitled "How Big is God?" The song said "He's big enough to rule His mighty universe, yet small enough to live within my heart." God indwells the bodies of believers according to I Corinthians 6:19, but He is also dwelling at the place of the *"highest stars."* Incredible!

In the passage quoted above from Psalm 139:7-10 it is clear that God's presence is in heaven and hell (the grave – *sheol*) at the same time.

When our daughter came up missing one Sunday after church, it was comforting to know that she was not away from the presence of God. She and a little friend had decided to walk to the store, but they got lost by going in the wrong direction. When we could not find her, we finally called the police. They located her and her friend about five miles from our church. Needless to say, we have a few anxious moments, yet we were reminded of the importance of God's presence, watching over them.

2. The universe and all that it contains is in God!

In Acts 17:24-28 the Apostle Paul is preaching in Athens about the one and only God. He explains the true God with these words:

"God that made the world and all things therein, seeing that He is Lord of heaven and earth, dwelleth not in temples made with hands; Neither is worshipped with men's hands, as though He needed any thing, seeing He giveth to all life, and breath, and all things; And hath made of one blood all nations of men for to dwell on all the face of the earth, and hath determined the times before appointed, and the bounds of their habitation; That they should seek the Lord, if haply they might feel after Him, and find Him, though He be not far from every one of us; For in Him we live, and move, and have our being; as certain also of your own poets have said, For we are also His offspring."

God's presence includes all the material and physical universe which He has created, including humanity. As far as you could travel into space, and even beyond that, there is God's presence. All the planets and stars are within His omnipresence. God said to Job in Job 38:4-7: *"Where wast thou when I laid the foundations of the earth? Declare, if thou hast understanding. Who hath laid the measures thereof, if thou* knowest? Or who hath stretched the line upon it? Whereupon are the foundations thereof fastened? Or who laid the corner stone thereof; When the morning stars sang together, and all the sons of God* (term in Old Testament refers to angels) *shouted for joy?"

God fixed the measurements of the earth. The earth is within the presence of God and its limitations are determined by Him. In Job 38:19 we read: *"Where is the way where light dwelleth? And as for darkness, where is the place thereof?"* In verse 24 He adds: *"By what way is the light parted, which scattereth the east wind upon the earth?"*

In Job 38:31-33 when we read these amazing statements: *"Canst thou bind the sweet influences of Pleiades, or loose the bands of Orion? Canst thou bring from Mazzaroth in his season? Or canst thou guide Arcturus with his sons? Knowest thou the ordinances of heaven? Canst thou set the dominion thereof in the earth?"*

God's presence is everywhere. The universe, including the constellations of stars, is within the scope of His presence and being constantly managed by Him.

One night while visiting friends in San Diego, California, we had the joy of sitting on top of their house which sits on the top of a mountain and looking at the stars that filled the sky. It was a very clear night and the view was spectacular. We were all enjoying the view when we began sharing about the greatness of God. We realized that all the stars we were admiring were within the majestic presence of God. That thought alone was rather overwhelming in the light of that beautiful sight. My friend shared: "Just think – that great God is also living in our bodies!" Were it not for clear Biblical teaching about God's presence in the believer, it was almost too incredible to believe!

3. God is separate from the universe in which He dwells!

Pantheism teaches that God is literally in everything. He is to be identified with the material universe. That is not taught in the Bible. In fact, the Bible makes it quite clear that God is separate from everything which He has made.

In the story of I Kings 19, Elijah the prophet is running away from Queen Jezebel and goes to a cave and hides there. The Lord speaks to him (recorded in I Kings 19:9) and asks: *"What doest thou here, Elijah?"* The Lord then invites him to view a display of nature's power, but reminds him of an important truth: The Lord is greater than the power of nature. Verse 11 speaks of a *"great and strong wind"* but the Lord was not in the wind. Then came an earthquake and these words: *"but the LORD was not in the earthquake."* Next came a fire, *"but the LORD was not in the fire."* God is not to be identified with even the forces of nature. Nature is NOT God! God is above nature and uses it to control and accomplish His purposes. Psalm 148:8 says: *"Fire, and hail; snow, and vapours; stormy wind fulfilling His word."*

As the Apostle Paul argued in Acts 17 (quoted above) God does not dwell in the bricks and stones. He is not in a table or in a chair. His presence is separate from the material universe which He created. All material things exist within the omnipresence of God, but He remains separate from them.

So, where is God? He is everywhere. His presence fills the whole universe. Jeremiah 23:24 says: *"Can any hide himself in secret places that I shall not see him? saith the LORD. Do not I fill heaven and earth? saith the LORD."*

For us to think that God is not near is simply a denial of Biblical truth. There is no place in this universe where we could go and not be in His presence. It is impossible for us to hide from God. Hebrews 4:13 reminds us: *"Neither is there any creature that is not manifest in His sight; but all things are naked and opened unto the eyes of Him with Whom we have to do."*

THE DIFFICULTIES OF THE OMNIPRESENCE OF GOD

To believe that God is omnipresent presents some problems to thinking people. There are at least three major difficulties that people encounter when trying to understand the Bible's teaching about the presence of God.

1. If God is everywhere, how can He be confined to one location such as heaven?

Psalm 11:4 says: *"The LORD is in His holy temple, the LORD's throne is in heaven; His eyes behold, His eyelids try, the children of men."*

Even though God's throne is in heaven, He is aware of the sons of men. Psalm 14:2 adds: *"The LORD looked down from heaven upon the children of men, to see if there were any that did understand, and seek God."* In I Kings 8:30 we read *"and hear Thou in heaven Thy dwelling place."*

But, if He is in heaven, how can He be everywhere at once? The answer that seems most plausible is that God is not everywhere present in the same sense. He is able to manifest Himself in special ways in different places. His presence in one place is not the same as His presence in another place, although we are not told what that difference is.

God is able to localize His presence by special revelation or visible evidence. He appeared in the pillar of fire by night and the cloud by day when He led the children of Israel through the wilderness. He appeared to Moses in the burning bush, and His special presence was represented by smoke filling the temple in the days of Isaiah. Not one of these figures (fire, cloud, smoke, burning bush, etc.) tells us all there is to know about the presence of God. They were simply visible manifestations of His presence. All of that which is His presence was not seen in any one of these symbols. Only a part of what is true about His presence is visible and known.

2. If God is everywhere, how could He dwell in a physical body?

This is a serious issue as it relates to the true identity of Yeshua (Jesus Christ). Is God able to localize Himself in a physical body, and still be everywhere at once? If He can give special manifestations of His presence in a given place (such as heaven or the Garden of Eden, etc.) could He not also do the same in a physical body? This seems like a more difficult question, but it also seems possible in the light of Biblical truth.

Colossians 1;19 says: *"For it pleased the Father that in Him should all fullness dwell."* The Greek text does not contain the words *"the Father."* It simply says that *"all the fullness was pleased to dwell in Him."* The term *"all the fullness"* seems to express the totality of God's Person and attributes, and according to this verse, that totality dwells in Jesus Christ. That this refers to the physical body of Yeshua is clear from Colossians 2:9: *"For in Him dwelleth all the fullness of the Godhead bodily."* This is a remarkable statement! Yeshua, the Messiah of Israel, is God manifest in the flesh as I Timothy 3:16 says: *"And without controversy great is the mystery of godliness: God was manifest in the flesh, justified in the Spirit, seen of angels, preached unto the Gentiles, believed on in the world, received up into glory."*

The Apostle John said in John 1:14 that the *"Word was made* (or became — Greek: *ginomai) flesh and dwelt among us and we beheld His glory."*

God's omnipresence was localized in the Person and body of Jesus Christ. He was not part of God, but all God! He was both God and man at the same time. Philippians 2:6 puts it this way: *"Who, being in the form* (Greek: *morphe) of God, thought it not robbery to be equal with God."* The word *"form"* refers to the exact essence or nature of something. Yeshua was and is God! I John 5:20 says of Him: *"This is the true God and eternal life."*

It is a mystery how God, Who is omnipresent, could localize Himself at all, whether in Old Testament manifestations, or in the Person of Yeshua HaMashiach (Jesus the Messiah). But the fact remains – He did it! As God, His abilities are far greater than our ability to understand!

3. If God is everywhere, how could anyone flee from His presence?

On several occasions we hear it said that someone is fleeing the presence of God. If He is everywhere at once, is not that an impossibility? The answer to that is both "yes" and "no." Naturally, we cannot hide or run away from God's presence and knowledge. However, from a human point of view, there is a sense in which we are doing the "running." We depart from conscious fellowship with Him.

In Job 1:12 we read: *"So Satan went forth from the presence of the LORD."* God's presence in this case is localized in heaven. He, no doubt, gives a visible manifestation of Himself. Satan leaves that visible manifestation of God's presence in heaven, even though there is no place where Satan can go that will escape the presence of God. Job 2:7 adds: *"So went Satan forth from the presence of the LORD."* It is that special manifestation of God's presence on His throne in heaven from which Satan leaves.

In Jonah 1:10 we read: *"For the men knew that he* (Jonah) *fled from the presence of the LORD, because he had told them."* This refers to Jonah's trying to run away from God. Of course, that is impossible in one sense – God is everywhere. However, Jonah is running away from the conscious presence of the Lord which he as a finite being had experienced. This fact of Jonah trying to run away from God and His declared will for his life is repeated several times (cf. verse 3).

We also learn in Genesis 4:16 that Cain *"went out from the presence of the LORD, and dwelt in the land of Nod, on the east of Eden."* The Lord's presence was localized and manifested in a special sense in the Garden of Eden. Back in Genesis 3:8 we also learn of Adam and Eve trying to hide themselves *"from the presence of the LORD God amongst the tress of the garden."* These passages illustrate how God's presence was manifested in a special way. It is clear that Adam and Eve could not hide from the presence of God, nor can we. He is everywhere. But, He can limit the manifestation of His presence whenever He chooses to do so.

WHY IS GOD'S PRESENCE SO COMFORTING TO THE BELIEVER?

To those who believe in Him, God's presence is the strength of their lives. God is there at all times to minister to us in our time of need. He cares and invites us to trust Him. Proverbs 3:5-6 says: *"Trust in the LORD with all thine heart, and lean not unto thine own understanding; In all thy ways acknowledge Him and He shall direct thy paths."* Consider prayerfully and carefully the marvelous blessings that arise from the fact of God's existence and presence.

1. God's presence gives stability!

In Psalm 16:8 David said: *"I have set the LORD always before me: because He is at my right hand, I shall not be moved."*

We live in a world of change where nothing seems to remain constant. The circumstances of life cause us to be insecure and unstable. We do not know from one day to the next what is going to happen. But, the Lord's presence is the stabilizing factor. As Deuteronomy 33:27 states, *"The eternal God is thy Refuge, and underneath are the everlasting arms."* What wonderful security! What stability!

Malachi 3:6 reminds us: *"For I am the LORD; I change not."* James 1:17 adds: *"Every good gift and every perfect gift is from above, and cometh down from the Father of lights, with Whom is no variableness, neither shadow of turning."* Although changes can at times be very threatening, there is One Who does not change and Whose presence gives stability to our lives. Our Lord can be trusted to bring stability to us when we feel so insecure. He is there as David said *"at my right hand."*

2. God's presence eliminates fear of dying!

Psalm 23:4 says: *"Yea, though I walk through the valley of the shadow of death, I will fear no evil: for Thou art with me; Thy rod and Thy staff they comfort me."*

The prospect of death never seems so real as that moment we are told by a physician that we have a terminal illness. It is a daily occurrence in the lives of thousands. I remember how frightened the woman who called me on the phone one day was. She was 42 years old and full of life, but her doctor had just informed her that she had serious cancer and had only about six months to live. She was scared and was crying uncontrollably. At a time like that, we need assurance that God is there and will be with us through the pain and tears. In the months ahead, her illness worsened, and she was finally hospitalized – never to return to her home and family. In the closing days before she died, her greatest joy was repeating the words of Psalm 23:4 to herself: *"I will fear no evil; for Thou art with me; Thy rod and Thy staff they comfort me."* In discovering the comfort of God's presence she became a blessing to all who visited her in those closing, agonizing days of her life on earth. She is now in the presence of the Lord Himself – her real home forever – read II Corinthians 5:1-8.

3. God's presence offers protection in times of crisis and difficulty!

We read in Isaiah 43:1-2 these wonderful words:

"But now thus saith the LORD that created thee, O Jacob, and He that formed thee, O Israel, Fear not: for I have redeemed thee, I have called thee by thy name; thou art Mine. When thou passest through the waters, I will be with thee; and through the rivers, they shall not overflow thee: when thou walkest through the fire, thou shalt not be burned; neither shall the flame kindle upon thee."

In Isaiah 43:5 we read: *"Fear not: for I am with thee."* The assurance of God's presence gives us great comfort in times of trial and crisis. Psalm 125:2 adds: *"As the mountains are round about Jerusalem, so the LORD is round about His people from henceforth even for ever."*

God takes care of Israel and has been with her through many times of trial and suffering. He never left their side. His presence was always there, surrounding them and protecting them.

4. God's presence encourages us in prayer!

We all have times when we pray and wonder if God is there. Does He hear us when we call? Psalm 145:18 says: *"The LORD is nigh unto all them that call upon Him, to all that call upon Him in truth."* Isaiah 55:6 says: *"Seek ye the LORD while He may be found, call ye upon Him while He is near."*

It is especially true in times of tears that the Lord's presence is comforting when we pray. Psalm 34:18 puts it like this: *"The LORD is nigh unto them that are of a broken heart; and saveth such as be of a contrite spirit."* Psalm 73:28 adds: *"But it is good for me to draw near to God; I have put my trust in the Lord GOD, that I may declare all Thy works."* James 4:8 says: *"Draw nigh to God and He will draw nigh to you."* Our prayer life becomes much more meaningful when we know of the nearness of God. He is there, listening and caring.

5. God's presence produces courage!

In Deuteronomy 31:8 Moses told Joshua about his role as leader of the children of Israel: *"And the LORD, He it is that doth go before thee; He will be with thee, He will not fail thee, neither forsake thee: fear not, neither be dismayed."* The LORD told Joshua directly in Joshua 1:9: *"Have not I commanded thee? Be strong and of a good courage; be not afraid, neither be thou dismayed: for the LORD thy God is with thee whithersoever thou goest."*

In Matthew 28:20 Yeshua said: *"and lo, I am with you always even to the end of the age."* Hebrews 13:5 says: *"I will never leave thee nor forsake thee."*

What wonderful assurance! There are many problems in life in which we must have courage and resolve. There are times of confrontation which cause most of us to back off and avoid conflict. Courage arises when we are confident of the Lord's will and presence.

God's existence and presence with us bring tremendous comfort. To know that He is there (at your right hand!) will help us in a difficult trial or time of sorrow. It will encourage us to pray to Him often, trusting Him to lead, protect, and give us courage to face what must inevitably come to all of us.

Stephen Charnock in his monumental work on the attributes of God speaks eloquently of the comfort of God's presence:

"It is not a piece of God is here and another parcel there, but God in His whole essence and perfections; in His wisdom to guide us, His power to protect and support us. His mercy to pity us, His fullness to refresh us, and His goodness to relieve us; He is ready to sparkle out in this or that perfection, as the necessities of His people require, and His own wisdom directs for His own honor; so that being not far from us in an excellency of His nature, we can quickly have recourse to Him upon any emergency, so that if we are miserable, we have the presence of His goodness; if we want direction, we have the presence of His wisdom; if we are weak, we have the presence of His power, and should we not rejoice in it, as a man doth in the presence of a powerful, wealthy, and compassionate friend?"

Chapter 7
How Powerful is God?

What can God do? One of the interesting things about people's understanding of God is how often they relate His power to the subject of physical healing. In the July 4, 1983, issue of TIME Magazine, a report on faith healing is given in the "Religion" section. The reporter penned these remarks: "It was impossible to discern which people might have been cured and which were subject only to passing psychological relief."

After a racquetball game, I went to the steam room to relax (and try to lose some more weight!). Several men filled that room and one man was telling his story about how God had recently healed his back. I became quite interested in his story as he began speaking eloquently of the mighty power of God. I asked him how his back was feeling now. He replied that it still hurt a little, but it was much better. I said: "It doesn't look as if God did a very good job!" He snapped back, "What are you, an unbeliever?" I said, "No, but I do wonder why God couldn't take all your soreness away if He really healed you."

The man replied, "God is powerful, but He can't do everything, you know!"

That kind of rationalizing, an attempt to explain apparent weaknesses in the healing ability of God, is simply not convincing. If the God of the Bible healed him, there would be no question about it! Most people are unaware of what the Bible really teaches about the power of God. They spend a lot of time trying to defend His apparent lack of concern and what seems to be (from their point of view) certain limitations of God. If He can do anything and everything, why does He not? Perhaps He is not as powerful as we think! Maybe the problem is our faith. It did not happen – maybe because we did not believe enough in His power. That is what many people who pray for healing, but do not experience it, are told by certain faith healers – "You didn't have enough faith, or you would have been healed."

Is God powerful enough to heal you? Can He put your marriage back together? Can He give you a better job? Could He give you more money? How about a new car? Can He stop nations from going to war against each other? Can He stop a storm or earthquake from happening in your community? Can He keep you from getting old? Can He cure cancer? It's easy to keep asking the questions.

A BIBLICAL DEFINITION

God is referred to in the Bible as the all-powerful or Almighty God. Revelation 19:6 declares (used in Handel's *Messiah*): *"Alleluia: for the Lord God omnipotent reigneth."* Omnipotence means that God is "all powerful" or that there is nothing that He cannot do that is consistent with His nature and purposes. He is frequently called *"the Almighty"* when referring to His works or His judgments. In describing His presence in the eternal state, the Book of Revelation calls Him *"Lord God Almighty"* – Revelation 21:22.

The residents of heaven sing praises to God continually, and they call Him *"Lord God Almighty* (Revelation 4:8; 11:17; 15:3)."* God refers to Himself as *"Almighty God"* when He appears to Abraham and announces His covenant with him (Genesis 17:1-2). The New

Testament word for *"Almighty"* appears ten times (Greek: *pantokrator*), and the primary Old Testament Hebrew word, *shaddai,* is used 48 times.

In putting together a Biblical definition of God's power we discover at least four important concepts in that definition. Each contributes to our understanding and will help us answer the question – "How powerful is God?"

1. God can do all things!

The Bible frequently affirms this truth, and usually does not try to answer all of the difficulties which such a statement can cause to our finite minds. For example, Job's reply (Job 42:2) to God's evaluation of his situation is: *"I know that Thou canst do every thing, and that no thought can be withholden from Thee."* While this declaration asserts the ability of God, it also suggests that God does what He wants to do. His purpose, therefore, controls His power. The question is not so much "Can he do it?" but "Will He do it?"

Yeshua gives this clear teaching about God's power when He answers the disciples' question about who can be saved if it is so hard for a rich man to enter the kingdom of heaven. Matthew 19:26 records his answer: *"With men this is impossible; but with God all things are possible."* Once again we are given the clue that while God's power can do all things in that they are *"possible,"* it does not automatically mean that He will do it.

A little boy about six years old fell down and scraped his knee right in front of me. He was running on the sidewalk of the church's educational building and was not looking at all the hazards of the ground below him. He was crying, and I immediately went over and picked him up. I took his handkerchief and carefully wiped the dirt and blood off of his knee. He looked up and asked, "Can God make the sore go away?" This was no time for a theological discourse, but here's what I said to that little boy: " He sure can, but He may want the sore to stay for a little while so you can remember why it happened and not do it again!" The boy seemed happy with that answer and off he went.

We need to state emphatically what the Bible teaches – that God can do anything and everything, but we must add: Everything that He *wants* to do!

2. Nothing is too hard for God to do!

There is nothing too hard or difficult for Him to do if He wants to do it. Consider the story of Genesis 18:9-15:

"And they said unto him, Where is Sarah thy wife? And he said, Behold, in the tent. And He said, I will certainly return unto thee according to the time of life; and lo, Sarah thy wife shall have a son. And Sarah heard it in the tent door, which was behind him. Now Abraham and Sarah were old and well stricken in age; and it ceased to be with Sarah after the manner of women. Therefore Sarah laughed within herself, saying, After I am waxed old shall I have pleasure, my lord being old also? And the LORD said unto Abraham, Wherefore did Sarah laugh, saying, Shall I of a surety bear a child, which am old? Is any thing too hard for the LORD? At the time appointed I will return unto thee, according to the time

of life, and Sarah shall have a son. Then Sarah denied, saying, I laughed not; for she was afraid. And He said, Nay, but thou didst laugh."

It is probably best if we don't criticize Sarah too harshly. We would have laughed also! If God told a woman today at the age of 89 years that she would have a baby one year from now, she might laugh also! The child that was born was named "Isaac" and that Hebrew name means "laughter." It is a reminder that nothing is too hard for the Lord to do. If He wants to do it, He can do it!

In Jeremiah 32:17 we read: *"Ah Lord GOD! behold, Thou hast made the heaven and the earth by Thy great power and stretched out arm, and there is nothing too hard for Thee."*

Several years ago Rabbi Harold Kushner wrote a best-selling book entitled "WHEN BAD THINGS HAPPEN TO GOOD PEOPLE." The author based his remarks upon the Biblical book of Job. He concluded that God must be limited – that there are some things He cannot do. Although this belief contradicts the clear teaching of the Bible, the author took a bold step. Assuming that the reluctance of God to do something, especially to stop evil from happening, shows His lack of concern, the author chose to believe that God is limited rather than believe that He does not care. The author's son died of progeria (aging disease). Before he died, Rabbi Kushner appeared on many talk shows and news broadcasts and appealed to people to pray for him. But, the conclusions he drew were both wrong. God cares and He can do anything He wants to do. His greater knowledge and purpose control His acts of power and love.

3. God will do what is consistent with His nature, character and purposes!

When people ask, "Can God make a rock that He cannot move?" they reveal their misunderstanding of Who God is and what He does do. Such a decision by God would be inconsistent for Him to do. These opinions are an insult to God Whose lovely character and mighty power will not stoop to such foolishness. He is under no obligation to prove His power to us beyond what He has already revealed in His Word! There are many things that God simply will not do. For example, Hebrews 6:18 states clearly that it is *"impossible for God to lie."*

When Yeshua was tempted by the devil in the wilderness, the devil tried to get Him to display His power and satisfy His need of hunger. Matthew 4:3 records the devil as saying: *"If Thou be the Son of God, command that these stones be made bread."* It is interesting to read the Greek text which uses a class condition of the "if clauses" that means "If and it is so." In other words, the devil knows that He is the Son of God. We might translate *"Since you are the Son of God...."*

Yeshua answered the devil in Matthew 4:4 by quoting from Deuteronomy 8:3: *"Man shall not live by bread alone, but by every word that proceedeth out of the mouth of God."* It is evident that there are things which the Lord will not do. They are contrary to His purposes. It is not a question of "Can He?" but of "Will He?" and even "Should He?"

Some of the things that God will not do or even cannot do include:

1. God cannot lie – *Titus 1:1-3;*
   Hebrews 6:18
2. God cannot be tempted by evil, nor
   does He tempt anyone else to do
   evil – *James 1:13*
3. God cannot deny Himself – *II*
   Timothy 2:13

4. God is never exhausted by the exercise of his power!

No matter how strong any one of us is,
we will get tired by the continual
exercise of strength. God never does.
Isaiah 40:28-31 clearly presents this
wonderful truth:

"Hast not thou known? Hast thou not
heard, that the everlasting God the
LORD, the Creator of the ends of the
earth, fainteth not, neither is weary?
There is no searching of His
understanding. He giveth power to the
faint, and to them that have no might
He increaseth strength. Even the
youths shall faint and be weary, and
the young men shall utterly fall. But
they that wait upon the LORD shall
renew their strength; they shall mount
up with wings as eagles; they shall run,

and not be weary; and they shall walk, and not faint."

God never gets tired and He doesn't need a nap either! Psalm 121:1-8 teaches:

"I will lift up mine eyes unto the hills, from whence cometh my help. My help cometh from the LORD, Which made heaven and earth. He will not suffer thy foot to be moved: He that keepeth thee will not slumber. Behold, He that keepeth Israel shall neither slumber nor sleep. The LORD is thy keeper: the LORD is thy shade upon thy right hand. The sun shall not smite thee by day, nor the moon by night. The LORD shall preserve thee from all evil: He shall preserve thy soul. The LORD shall preserve thy going out and thy coming in from this time forth, and even forevermore."

In defining the omnipotence of God we have shared at least four concepts:

    1. God can do all things.
    2. Nothing is too hard for God to do.

3. God will do that which is consistent with His nature, character, and purposes.
4. God is never exhausted by the exercise of His power.

Definitions are good, but the impact of those definitions is best felt when we see the actual display of God's power. Just what kind of things does God do which prove what our definition has told us?

EVIDENCES OF GOD'S POWER

People want proof. You cannot just tell them – you must show them. God realizes that more than we do, and He has often revealed His mighty power to people on earth. He has shown us that His power is behind all of what we see in the material universe as well as in the processes of natural law. He has frequently interrupted the natural and performed the supernatural. We will now draw your attention to six areas in which God has displayed His mighty power.

1. The Creation of the Universe

Romans 1:20 makes this bold statement about the creation of the universe: *"For the invisible things of Him from the creation of the world are clearly seen, being understood by the things that are made, even His eternal power and Godhead; so that they are without excuse."*

With one look at the created universe one quickly understands something of the mighty power of God – it is awesome and overwhelming! Words are inadequate to describe such power. To try to explain its presence by natural law is hopeless. The telescopic and microscopic worlds are wonders to behold and are clear testimony to the enormous power and genius of the Creator. Bible writers attest to this fact on many occasions as did the prophet Jeremiah (10:12): *"He hath made the earth by His power, He hath established the world by His wisdom, and hath stretched out the heavens by His discretion."*

Psalm 8:3 adds: *"When I consider Thy heavens, the work of Thy fingers, the moon and the stars, which Thou hast ordained."* Creation is described as the "finger play" of God! Psalm 19:1 says: *"The heavens declare the glory of God; and the firmament* (expanse) *sheweth His handiwork."* Psalm 102:25 adds: *"Of old hast Thou laid the foundation of the earth: and the heavens are the work of Thy hands."*

What more do we need to see? The galaxies are incredible reminders of the greatness and power of our God!

2. The Processes of Nature

Jeremiah 10:13 states: *"When he uttereth His voice, there is a multitude of waters in the heavens, and He causeth the vapors to ascend from the ends of the earth; He maketh lightnings with rain, and bringeth forth the wind out of His treasures."*

Psalm 104:10-24 speaks eloquently of the Lord's power in the processes of nature:

"He sendeth the springs into the valleys, which run among the hills. They give drink to every beast of the field: the wild asses quench their thirst. By them shall the fowls of the heaven have their

habitation, which sing among the branches. He watereth the hills from His chambers: the earth is satisfied with the fruit of Thy works. He causeth the grass to grow for the cattle, and herb for the service of man: that He may bring forth food out of the earth; And wine that maketh glad the heart of man, and oil to make his face to shine, and bread which strengtheneth man's heart. The trees of the LORD are full of sap; the cedars of Lebanon, which He hath planted; Where the birds make their nests: as for the stork the fir trees are her home. The high hills are a refuge for the wild goats; and the rocks for the conies. He appointed the moon for seasons: the sun knoweth his going down. Thou makest darkness, and it is night: wherein all the beasts of the forest do creep forth. The young lions roar after their prey, and seek this meat from God. The sun ariseth, they gather themselves together, and lay them down in their dens. Man goeth forth unto his work and to his labor until the evening. O LORD, how manifold are Thy works! In wisdom hast Thou made them all: the earth is full of Thy riches."

All of nature speaks of the majesty and power of God! Psalm 104:30 says: *"Thou sendest forth Thy Spirit, they are created: and Thou renewest the face of the earth."*

3. The Laws of the Universe

Why do the planets not collide? Why do objects fall to the earth and not out into space? We know that certain laws operate behind the scenes to keep the universe functioning properly. The Bible teaches that God is manifesting His power in these laws, which we have all learned to accept as facts.

Colossians 1:17 says concerning God the Son: *"And He is before all things, and by Him all things consist* (hold together). *"* Hebrews 1:3 adds: *"Who being the brightness of His glory, and the express image of His Person, and upholding all things by the word of His power, when He had by Himself purged our sins, sat down on the right hand of the Majesty on high."* God's power is sustaining all the physical laws of the universe. You may not agree that God is the One doing it, but something or someone is! God inquires of Job in Job

38:33: *"Knowest thou the ordinances* (laws) *of heaven? Canst thou set the dominion thereof in the earth?"* God spoke to Job about His power in the laws of the universe in order to challenge Job to trust Him completely in the times of suffering which he had endured. In Job 38:4-7 we read:

"Where wast thou when I laid the foundations of the earth? declare, if thou hast understanding. Who hath laid the measures thereof, if thou knowest? Or who hath stretched the line upon it? Whereupon are the foundations thereof fastened? Or what laid the corner stone thereof; When the morning stars sang together, and all the sons of God (angels) *shouted for joy?"*

4. The Plagues of Egypt

One of the great displays of the power of God happened in Egypt over 3000 years ago. When you visit Egypt today, you are constantly confronted with the story of Israel's presence there. They still remember! While many question the validity of what happened or we might say the extent to which events described in the Bible really occurred, everyone agrees that something unusual did indeed happen. Many of us are convinced that amazing miracles and demonstrations of God's power actually took place.

The entire history of the Old Testament is filled with continual reminders and admonitions of how God redeemed Israel out of Egypt. In the Book of Deuteronomy, fathers are told to instruct their children about what happened in Egypt. In Deuteronomy 6:21-22 it says:

"Then thou shalt say unto thy son, We were Pharaoh's bondmen in Egypt; and the LORD brought us out of Egypt with a mighty hand: and the LORD shewed signs and wonders, great and sore, upon Egypt, upon Pharaoh, and upon all his household, before our eyes."

These *"signs and wonders"* included ten plagues. The magicians of Pharaoh were able to counterfeit the first two plagues (waters turned into blood and an infestation of frogs) according to Exodus 7:22 and 8:7, but when the third plague (lice) hit, they could not duplicate it and said to Pharoah: *"This is the finger of God (Exodus 8:19)."* They began to realize the awesome power of God, and all their occultic magic and demonic involvement could not compete with the mighty power of God.

The interesting thing about the Egyptian encounter with the power of God is that it was predicted by God before it occurred. In Exodus 7:3 God said to Moses: *"And I will harden Pharaoh's heart, and multiply My signs and My wonders in the land of Egypt."* In Exodus 9:16 we learn God's purpose in such a demonstration of His power to Pharoah: *"And in very deed for this cause have I raised thee up, for to shew in thee My power; and that My Name may be declared throughout all the earth."*

After Israel crossed the Red Sea (literally the Gulf of Aqaba) through another tremendous display of God's mighty power, God destroyed Pharaoh and his army in the sea. Moses wrote this song of victory to the Lord (Exodus 15:1-8):

"Then sang Moses and the children of
Israel this song unto the LORD, and
spake, saying, I will sing unto the
LORD, for He hath triumphed
gloriously; the horse and his rider hath
He thrown into the sea. The LORD is
my strength and song, and He is
become my salvation: He is my God,
and I will prepare Him an habitation;
my father's God, and I will exalt Him.
The LORD is a man of war: the LORD is
His Name. Pharaoh's chariots and his
host hath He cast into the sea: his
chosen captains also are drowned in the
Red sea. The depths have covered them:
they sank into the bottom as a stone.
Thy right hand, O LORD, is become
glorious in power: Thy right hand, O
LORD, hath dashed in pieces the enemy.
And in the greatness of Thine excellency
Thou has overthrown them that rose up
against Thee; Thou sentest forth Thy
wrath, which consumed them as
stubble. And with the blast of Thy
nostrils the waters were gathered
together, the floods stood upright as an
heap, and the depths were congealed in
the heart of the sea."

Exodus 15:11-13 continues: "Who is like
unto Thee, O LORD, among the gods?

*Who is like Thee, glorious in holiness,
fearful in praises, doing wonders?
Thou stretchedst out Thy right hand,
the earth swallowed them. thou in Thy
mercy hast led forth the people which
Thou hast redeemed: Thou hast guided
them in Thy strength unto Thy holy
habitation."*

No doubt about it – the plagues of Egypt,
the crossing of the Gulf of Aqaba into the
land of Midian (Saudi Arabia today) and
the drowning of the Egyptian army in
the sea – are sensational and mighty
examples of the awesome power of
Almighty God!

5. The Miracles of Yeshua

It was well known in the first century AD
that a Jewish man in Israel was able to
perform miracles. He could heal the
sick, calm a stormy sea, feed 5000
people with one boy's lunch, walk on
water, and even raise the dead! Flavius
Josephus (one time the Commander of
the Galilean Forces) was the Jewish
historian who wrote of the events of the
first century AD. His monumental work,
"ANTIQUITIES AND WARS OF THE
JEWS," speaks briefly about Yeshua and

his abilities. In Chapter 3 we read his analysis:

"Now there was about this time Jesus, a wise man, if it be lawful to call him a man; for he was a doer of wonderful works, a teacher of such men as receive the truth with pleasure. He drew over to him both many of the Jews and many of the Gentiles. He was the Christ. And when Pilate, at the suggestion of the principal men amongst us, had condemned him to the cross, those that loved him at the first did not forsake him, for he appeared to them alive again the third day, as the divine prophets had foretold these and ten thousand other wonderful things concerning him. And the tribe of Christians, so named from him, are not extinct at this day."

There are several scholars who doubt the authenticity of all of his remarks. But, the reference that says *"a doer of wonderful works"* is probably quite accurately stated.

In John 21:25 in the New Testament we read these words concerning the miracles of Yeshua: *"And there are also many other things which Jesus did, the which, if they should be written every one, I suppose that even the world itself could not contain the books that should be written."*

John 20:30-31 states the purpose behind the miracles of Yeshua: *"And many other signs truly did Jesus in the presence of His disciples, which are not written in this book; But these are written, that ye might believe that Jesus is the Christ, the Son of God; and that believing ye might have life through His Name."*

At the Jewish celebration of Shavuot Pentecost) mentioned in Acts 2, Simon Peter spoke of the miracles of Yeshua in Acts 2:22: *"Ye men of Israel, hear these words; Jesus of Nazareth, a man approved of God among you by miracles and wonders and signs, which God did by Him in the midst of you, as ye yourselves also know."*

Although miracles are a demonstration of God's power (If they are supernatural!) they do not always convince people. Though many saw His miracles performed, they still did not believe His claims. Perhaps He was a magician, or worse yet, an instrument of satanic power. These miracles were evidence of His claim to be the Messiah of Israel. We might call them His credentials. Isaiah 35:5-6 speaks of how the miracles will identify the Messiah: *"Then the eyes of the blind shall be opened, and the ears of the deaf shall be unstopped. Then shall the lame man leap as an hart, and the tongue of the dumb sing..."*

6. The Resurrection of Yeshua

Talk about power! Ephesians 1:19-20 wants us to know *"what is the exceeding greatness of His power to us-ward who believe, according to the working of His mighty power, which He wrought in Christ, when He raised Him from the dead, and set Him at His own right hand in the heavenly places."*

Yeshua said in John 10:18: *"No man taketh it from Me, but I lay it down of Myself. I have power to lay it down, and I have power to take it again."*

Romans 1:4 says of Yeshua: *"declared to be the Son of God with power, according to the spirit of holiness, by the resurrection from the dead."*

The Apostle Paul wrote in Philippians 3:10: *"that I may know Him and the power of His resurrection."*

Christianity is built upon the historical fact that Yeshua (Jesus) rose from the dead. If He did not, true Christianity would collapse. To the believer, the resurrection is the great demonstration of the power of God.

I was trying to comfort a young wife whose husband had been killed in an automobile accident, when she asked: *"Did the resurrection really happen?"* There was a seriousness and concern in her question that day which remains with me today. The only comfort that sustained her at that time was that which sustains all true believers in our Lord – and that is the hope of the resurrection. If God's power raised Yeshua from the dead, then He is capable of raising all of us from the dead. It is as simple as that!

The evidences of God's power in the past should build our confidence in the power of God for the future. The Bible teaches that God's power will be displayed once again as it was in Egypt over 3000 years ago. This time it will affect the entire world, not just one country.

There is going to be catastrophic events that can only be explained by the mighty power of God. The last book of the Bible, Revelation, records these events. Revelation 16:9 reveals that the people of the earth will know that God is showing His power through some awful plagues; but, they will not repent and believe in Him. That is the tragedy of human nature. Our pride and selfishness keep us from knowing and believing in the One and only God, the God of power!

WHY WE NEED GOD'S POWER!

Assuming we believe that God's power is real and available, why do we need it in our lives? That is somewhat like asking whether grass needs water to grow! It should be obvious that we need help of an extraordinary kind. In a narcissistic society where people begin and end with themselves, the poverty of human solutions and pursuits becomes more evident with each passing year. Our powerlessness to change the moral decay and meaninglessness of our lives is all too apparent. We need help!

The man sitting in my office was the epitome of despair and disappointment. All of his life he was in charge (or so he thought!) but things never turned out the way he wanted. His marriage broke up, his children turned away from him and his values, his job was given to a younger man, and his ideals were destroyed before his eyes. He never needed anyone or anything until now. He thought he could manage effectively and produce consistently over the years of his life. Everything now seemed like a boy's fantasy. He asked me, "What do I do now?" When I suggested he needed God's help and power, he said, "What good will that do?" The following discussion is an attempt to answer that question.

1. Human limitations need God's power!

It is a shock to a man who has enjoyed athletic prowess and physical strength most of his life to discover his weakness. The old knees do not move as they once did. He gets out of breath before the game is over and his body aches more than ever. He can't run as fast or as long, and his quickness is gone. Younger men give him that condescending smile that suggests he is too old and should maybe join the wheelchair crowd!

The prophet Isaiah spoke of our need for God's power and strength – simply because of our human limitations. We read in Isaiah 40:28-31 these encouraging words:

"Hast thou not known? Hast thou not heard, that the everlasting God, the LORD, the Creator of the ends of the earth, fainteth not, neither is weary? There is no searching of His understanding. He giveth power to the faint; and to them that have no might He increaseth strength. Even the youths shall faint and be weary, and the young men shall utterly fall. But they that wait upon the LORD shall renew their strength; they shall mount up with wings as eagles; they shall run,

and not be weary; and they shall walk, and not faint."

The Apostle Paul wrote In II Corinthians 12:7-10 the following:

"And lest I should be exalted above measure through the abundance of the revelations, there was given to me a thorn in the flesh, the messenger of Satan to buffet me, lest I should be exalted above measure. For this thing I besought the Lord thrice, that it might depart from me. And He said unto me, My grace is sufficient for thee: for My strength is made perfect in weakness. Most gladly therefore will I rather glory in my infirmities, that the power of Christ may rest upon me. Therefore I take pleasure in infirmities, in reproaches, in necessities, in persecutions, in distresses for Christ's sake: for when I am weak, then am I strong."

God's strength and power are greatly needed in our times of weakness. It is something special to know His power when you are faced with your limitations.

Ephesians 3:20 says: *"Now unto Him that is able to do exceeding abundantly above all that we ask or think, according to the power that worketh in us."* His power can do more than we can ask or think. Strange it is that we do not call upon Him more! Our pride and self-sufficiency prevent that until a few trying experiences of defeat point out our need. The need has been there all along, but our self-confident inability to admit weakness keeps us from depending upon God and His power. Paul wrote in Philippians 4:13: *"I can do all things through Christ which strengtheneth me."* Inward spiritual power is much greater than outward physical strength. Our limitations are reminders of our need for God's power.

Samson was a man who learned the secret of God's power – the hard way! His hair was an outward symbol of God's power, and when it was cut, his great strength was gone. His enemies, the Philistines, made a great feast in the temple of their god to celebrate their apparent victory over Samson, who had defeated them on so many occasions. Samson was mocked in their presence. They had gouged out his eyes and chained him. Samson made one last appeal to God to display His power and destroy the Philistines. After asking a young boy to guide his hands toward the pillars of the temple, he called on the Lord and pushed those pillars down, and the entire structure collapsed killing about 3000 people, including Samson himself.

2. Our Salvation requires God's power!

We cannot save ourselves from sin, death, and hell. It takes the power of God! The gospel of the Messiah is called in Romans 1:16 – *"the power of God unto salvation to everyone that believeth."*

It is the mystery of Christianity that requires a person to trust the power of God rather than depend upon human performance or self-worth. One man said to me: "If it's free, I don't think it's worth having; and if I can't earn it, I don't want it!" This was his replay to my description of the salvation which God offers – it must be believed, and it cannot be earned nor do we deserve it.

The disciples of Yeshua were perplexed over His remarks about the difficulty that rich men have in being converted. He said that it was easier for a camel to go through the eye of a weaver's needle than for a rich man to enter the kingdom of God (Matthew 19:24). After that remark, the disciples asked, *"Who then can be saved?"* The answer of Yeshua was: *"With men this is impossible; but with God all things are possible."*

3. God's promises need God's power!

The power of God is needed to back up the promises of God. What assurance do we have that He can do what He claims if He does not have the power or the ability to do them?

Romans 4:20-21 speaks of God's promise to Abraham about having a child in his old age: *"He staggered not at the promise of God through unbelief; but was strong in faith, giving glory to God; And being fully persuaded that, what He had promised, He was able also to perform."*

Abraham's confidence had to be in the power of God for that promise to be fulfilled. The only way he (age 99) and his wife, Sarah (age 89) who was barren, were going to have a child is if a miracle was performed by the power of God. God's power is behind His promises.

4. Our eternal security needs God's power!

I Peter 1:5 says: *"Who are kept by the power of God through faith unto salvation ready to be revealed in the last time."* Romans 8:38-39 makes a powerful point about our security: *"For I am persuaded, that neither death, nor life, nor angels, nor principalities, nor powers, not things present, nor things to come, nor height, nor depth, nor any other creature, shall be able to separate us from the love of God, which is in Christ Jesus our Lord."*

That's what I call security! What can separate us? Absolutely nothing! God's power to keep us prevents it.

A young girl shared with me her insecurity. She had doubts about her salvation and whether or not the Lord would ever forgive her. Her father had left her and her mother for another woman. She was eight years old at the time. Her mother, an alcoholic, left her with others for many years. Her boyfriend had just broken up with her. All of her "security blankets" were gone! She now had great doubts about her relationship to God. I shared with her the wonderful words of Yeshua in John 10:28-29: *"And I give unto them eternal life; and they shall never perish, neither shall any man pluck them out of My hand. My Father, which gave them Me, is greater than all; and no man is able to pluck them out of the Father's hand."* I also told her the words of Hebrews 13:5 where our Lord says: *"I will never leave thee, nor forsake thee."*

We need God's power for everything, although sometimes it takes a tragedy or heartache to show that fact to us. One friend I know never saw his need for God's power until his wife died. Then he went to pieces, and soon learned his need for God's power. We need God's power just to make it through the day, especially in our relationships with people. We need His power to overcome sinful habits and to live an abundant, joyful, and fruitful Christian life. We need His power to witness to others, and to use our spiritual gifts effectively for His glory. Without God's power, we soon reveal our weaknesses and faults.

Chapter 8
What Does God Know?

Does God know everything? I John 3:20 says that God knows all things. That can be very threatening as well as reassuring, depending on what is going on in your life at the time.

Sometimes I wonder if God knows what I am doing or what I am thinking about doing. One sleepy summer day as I was lying on the grass looking up at a clear blue sky with a few scattered white clouds passing by, I began to think about what God knows. I picked up a dandelion and proceeded to remove the leaves one by one. As I considered getting something cold to drink, I thought to myself – "I wonder if God knows what I want to do." As I picked the leaves off that dandelion, I said, after the first leaf, "I'm going to get that drink." The next leaf caused me to say, "I'm not going to get that drink." I found myself saying to God, "I'll bet You wonder how this is going to turn out, don't You?" After using up all my leaves, I started laughing. I know that God even knew I would pick off the leaves of that dandelion and wonder about whether or not I would get a drink. In case you are wondering, I got the drink, and God knew that I would!

Watching a replay of a football game on television reminds me somewhat of God's omniscience. He knows all things, even what is going to happen next. That is what I knew while watching the replay because I saw the original, live performance of that football play.

What is Included in the "All Things" That God Knows?

1. The design and function of the material universe is known to Him!

The word "all" includes the intangible things like wisdom. Job 28:23 says: *"God understandeth the way thereof, and He knoweth the place thereof."* God knows the material universe in a way none of us does. Psalm 147:4 states: *"He telleth the number of the stars; He calleth them all by their names."* That alone is an incredible insight into the infinite knowledge of God. In Job 38:33, the LORD God says to Job: *"Knowest thou the ordinances of heaven? Canst thou set the dominion thereof in the earth?"* Obviously not!

2. The reproduction of wild goats is known by Him!

He continues to question Job in Job 39:1-2 and says: *"Knowest thou the time when the wild goats of the rock bring forth? Or canst thou mark when the hinds do calve? Canst thou number the months that they fulfill? Or knowest thou the time when they bring forth?"*

3. The details of birds falling and the number of hairs on our heads are both known to Him!

Matthew 10:29-30 reminds us that God knows when a sparrow falls to the ground and that the number of hairs on our heads is known to him. What details! God knows all things!

4. The past and the future are known by Him!

God knows our days even before we experience them and is intimately acquainted with us even before we are born. Psalm 139:16 says: *"Thine eyes did see my substance, yet being unperfect; and in Thy book all my members were written, which in continuance were fashioned, when as yet there was none of them."* The LORD says in Jeremiah 1:5: *"Before I formed thee in the belly, I knew thee; and before thou camest forth out of the womb I sanctified thee, and I ordained thee a prophet unto the nations."* Isaiah 46:10 says: *"Declaring the end from the beginning, and from ancient times the things that are not yet done, saying, My counsel shall stand, and I will do all My pleasure."*

5. He knows all about every one of us!

Job 26:6 says: *"Hell is naked before Him, and destruction hath no covering."* Psalm 33:13-15 adds: *"The LORD looketh from heaven; He beholdeth all the sons of men. From the place of His habitation He looketh upon all the inhabitants of the earth. he fashioneth their hearts alike; He considereth all their works."*

One of the greatest passages in the Bible concerning the omniscience of God is Psalm 139:1-6:

"O LORD, Thou hast searched me, and known me. Thou knowest my downsitting and mine uprising, Thou understandest my thought afar off. Thou compasseth my path and my lying down, and art acquainted with all my ways. For there is not a word in my tongue, but, lo, O LORD, Thou knowest it altogether. Thou hast beset me behind and before, and laid Thine hand upon me. Such knowledge is too wonderful (incomprehensible) *for me; it is high, I cannot attain unto it."*

God's knowledge of us is all-inclusive – nothing is left out. As a young boy of ten, I was greatly tempted to steal a certain item out of a store in our neighborhood. It was something I really wanted. I argued to myself that they would not miss the item and could afford the loss. What bothered my conscience was the teaching of my parents that God knows all things. His knowledge of what I was thinking kept me that day from stealing. Though I have failed Him many times since, I am still aware today (even more so!) that there is nothing I do, say, or think that escapes His knowledge.

When the apostles of our Lord met to replace Judas who hanged himself, they faced a difficult decision. There were two men among the disciples of Jesus who met the qualifications: Joseph, called Barsabas, with a surname of Justus, and a man named Matthias. They prayed to God and Acts 1:24 records what they said: *"Thou, Lord, which knowest the hearts of all men, shew whether of these two Thou hast chosen."* Then, they cast lots (a method of voting) and Matthias was chosen.

Hebrews 4:13 says: *"Neither is there any creature that is not manifest in His sight; but all things are naked and opened unto the eyes of Him with Whom we have to do."* Proverbs 15:3 states clearly: *"The eyes of the LORD are in every place, beholding the evil and the good."* He sees it all and knows it all!

6. He knows who is really a believer or not!

Psalm 1:6 says: *"For the LORD knoweth the way of the righteous: but the way of the ungodly shall perish."* Also, in II Timothy 2:19 we read: *"The Lord knoweth them that are His."*

Yeshua said in John 10:27: *"My sheep hear My voice, and I know them, and they follow Me."* In John 2:23-25 we see the fact of the Lord's knowledge about believers being declared:

"Now when He was in Jerusalem in the Passover, in the feast day, many believed in His Name, when they saw the miracles which He did. But Yeshua (Jesus) *did not commit Himself unto them, because He knew all men, and needed not that any should testify of man: for He knew what was in man."* The word *"commit"* is the same Greek word as the word *"believe."* They responded to the miracles that He did, but our Lord reveals that they were not genuine believers in His true identity.

God knows all things from beginning to end. He is not surprised by any turn of events. The circumstances of our lives are all known to Him, not only in terms of the event that is happening, but also in terms of why it happens.

HOW DOES HIS KNOWLEDGE AFFECT US?

When we say that God knows everything, it has some practical implications as to what we think, say, and do. Much of our immaturity is directly traceable to our misunderstanding or misapplication of God's omniscience. To know that He knows is the beginning of knowledge itself. Proverbs 2:3-6 makes this clear:

"Yea, if thou criest after knowledge, and liftest up thy voice for understanding; If thou seekest her as silver, and searchest for her as for his treasures; Then shalt thou understand the fear of the LORD, and find the knowledge of God. For the LORD giveth wisdom; out of His mouth cometh knowledge and understanding."

Proverbs 9:10 states: *"The fear of the LORD is the beginning of wisdom: and the knowledge of the Holy* (One) *is understanding."*

It reveals the need for HONESTY!

Nothing so affects the honesty of the soul as the firm conviction that what a person is hiding is known to others. Our character is what God knows us to be, but our reputation is only what people think we are. God knows what we are really like, so why be dishonest before Him? Do we really believe He does not see what we do or know what we say? This is a sobering matter: Job 11:11 says: *"For He knoweth vain men: He seeth wickedness also; will He not then consider it?"* Psalm 44:21 adds: *"Shall not God search this out? For He knoweth the secrets of the heart."* Nothing in the deep recesses of our hearts escapes His knowledge.

King David learned that lesson the hard way. He committed adultery with Bathsheba and arranged the death of her husband. He thought that no one knew. Then, the prophet Nathan exposed him. In Psalm 51:6, David wrote: *"Behold, Thou desirest truth in the inward parts; and in the hidden part Thou shalt make me to know wisdom."*

Stop deceiving yourself about your sinful thoughts and secret deeds – God knows! Psalm 69:5 declares: *"O God,*

Thou knowest my foolishness; and my sins are not hid from Thee." Psalm 90:8 adds: *"Thou hast set our iniquities before Thee, our secret sins in the light of Thy countenance."* Proverbs 15:3 reminds us: *"The eyes of the LORD are in every place, beholding the evil and the good."*

In Joshua 7 there is an important story about honesty and confession. Joshua had just begun the campaign to defeat the Canaanite strongholds in the land of Israel and take possession as God had commanded. At the city of Ai (a small place with few inhabitants) the people of Israel were defeated and shocked. Joshua 7:5 says: *"the hearts of the people melted and became as water."* The problem? A man named Achan had sinned against the Lord by taking some of the pagan spoils which God said to destroy. He hid them in his tent, thinking that no one would know. But God knows! In an incredible display of God's knowledge, lots were cast to determine the tribe, the family, the particular household, and finally the guilty person. Achan was exposed, and Joshua said in Joshua 7:19: *"My son, give, I pray thee, glory to the LORD God of Israel, and make confession unto Him; and tell me now what thou hast done; hide it not from me."* It clearly glorifies God when we confess our sins instead of trying to hide or cover them. Proverbs 28:13 states: *"He that covereth his sins shall not prosper: but whoso confesseth and forsaketh them shall have mercy."* Our refusal to be honest before God often affects others (as in the case of Achan's sin and Israel's defeat), even though we think it will not because no one knows. But God knows!

It reveals the need for ACCEPTANCE!

Most of us think that if people really knew what we are like, they would no longer accept us and love us; so we keep "putting on." Because we want their approval, we try to impress others with what we do, as well as what we would not do. The need for acceptance is powerful in all of us.

Ephesians 1:6 says: *"To the praise of the glory of His grace, wherein He hath made us accepted in the Beloved* (Beloved One – referring to Yeshua!). *"* Through our faith in Yeshua as our

Messiah and Lord, we are accepted by God. Yet, He knows what we are like! In Psalm 103:8-14 we learn that God knows us quite well:

"The LORD is merciful and gracious, slow to anger, and plenteous in mercy. He will not always chide: neither will He keep His anger forever. He hath not dealt with us after our sins; nor rewarded us according to our iniquities. For as the heaven is high above the earth, so great is His mercy toward them that fear Him. As far as the east is from the west, so far hath He removed our transgressions from us. Like as a father pitieth his children, so the LORD pitieth them that fear Him. For He knoweth our frame; He remembereth that we are dust."

He knows all about us, but He still loves and accepts us – thanks to His patience and mercy!

Jenny was a girl who never felt accepted by her parents, who were perfectionists. She could never measure up and got into the practice of lying in order to make people accept her and respond to her. She was greatly troubled that people would find out about her failures and faults and reject her. Jenny had some learning disabilities that made her feel quite insecure in most social settings. Fear, hurt, bitterness, suspicion, jealousy, insecurity – all these emotions and more were her daily diet. When she learned that God knows all about her, including all that she was hiding inside, she became very fearful at first. She thought God, therefore, must reject her if He really knows her. After being assured that such was not the case, since God's knowledge brings God's loving understanding, she slowly became excited about what God has said in His Word. She began to relax in the full acceptance of God and His love for her, and her relationships with people began to thrive and develop. God's knowledge can be frightening if we are trying to hide, but wonderful if we know His love and forgiveness.

It reveals the need for TRUST!

Because God knows all things, He can be trusted. We can depend upon Him in time of trial and need. A greater knowledge of God results in a greater trust in God. The more we know about

God, the more we want to trust Him. It is very often the limited understanding of God or the myths people believe about God that makes them turn away from Him or be fearful to trust Him. There are several important areas of our lives where the knowledge of God leads us to trust Him. The following represents only a few of the reasons we can depend upon Him:

1. PRAYER

It is the spiritual air we breathe and it is vital to our relationship with God. Some of us ignore prayer, to our detriment, and others simply do not believe in it. many do not know how to pray. Even the disciples asked Yeshua in Luke 11:1: *"Lord, teach us to pray, as John also taught his disciples."* We all need to learn how to pray.

A fundamental need in prayer is that of faith or trust in God. Yeshua said in Matthew 21:22: *'And all things, whatsoever ye shall ask in prayer, believing, ye shall receive."* But can God be trusted? Will He give you whatever you ask? When will He do it?

Does He really hear your prayers when He has so many others to hear?

First of all, our heavenly Father knows how we pray and why we pray. We are not deceiving Him. Yeshua revealed this in Matthew 6:5-8:

"And when thou prayest, thou shalt not be as the hypocrites are: for they love to pray standing in the synagogues and in the corners of the streets, that they may be seen of men. Verily I say unto you, They have their reward. But thou, when thou prayest, enter into thy closet, and when thou hast shut thy door, pray to thy Father which is in secret; and thy Father which seeth in secret shall reward thee openly. But when ye pray, use not vain repetitions, as the heathen do: for they think that they shall be heard for their much speaking. Be not ye therefore like unto them: for your Father knoweth what things ye have need of before ye ask Him."

We observe that private prayer is better than public prayer, where the constant temptation exists to be seen or heard by others. We learn that *"in secret"* our motives and requests are clearly seen by God and, with no one but Him to talk to or be seen by, we have a greater chance of being rewarded. We also do not need to repeat the same words or chants over and over again, as many pagan religions encourage. Though we may ask God about something again on another day (and should!), we do not need to repeat ourselves within the context of one prayer. The reason? God knows what we need before we ask Him.

So, why pray at all?

For one reason – God commanded us to do it. Another reason – there is more to prayer than informing God of things we are not sure He knows. The fact is, God already knows our needs, but that eliminates neither the joy of talking to Him about them nor the need of getting our emotions clarified by talking to God. Our greater need may be patience, peace, or trust – not simply receiving the answer to our first request. God's knowledge encourages us to pray because we know that He knows our real needs. We don't – we may think we do, but if we are truthful – we don't!

Yeshua said in Matthew 6:31-34 these words:

"Therefore take no thought, saying, What shall we eat? Or, What shall we drink? Or, Wherewithal shall we be clothed? For all these things do the Gentiles seek: for your heavenly Father knoweth that ye have need of all these things. But seek ye first the kingdom of God, and His righteousness; and all these things shall be added unto you. Take therefore no thought for the morrow: for the morrow shall take thought for the things of itself. Sufficient unto the day is the evil thereof."

In the above passage, God's knowledge eliminates worry and anxiety about what to eat, drink, or wear, and even about what tomorrow will be like. God can be trusted – so relax! This special sermon by Yeshua (called the Sermon on the Mount) emphasizes true righteousness as compared with outward, external religious activity. Material needs and concerns about tomorrow do not represent the real priorities. God already knows about these matters. We need to seek first His kingdom and righteousness. The point is that God's knowledge not only eliminates undue concern for temporal matters, but also helps us to concentrate on the real priorities because we know He will take care of our minor needs due to His knowledge of them. The real problem in many of our prayers, therefore, is concentration on the physical rather than the spiritual, the lesser priority over the greater one – all of which ignores the vast knowledge of God. Instead of trusting, we begin to worry. Once again, the root of our problem is a misunderstanding or misapplication of Who God is and what He can do!

2. SUFFERING

The knowledge of God can really help if you are presently going through some difficult times. When you are hurting, you often wonder if God knows, and, most of all, if He cares. Psalm 31:7 speaks of God's knowledge in times of stress: *"I will be glad and rejoice in His mercy: for Thou hast considered my trouble; Thou hast known my soul in adversities."* In Psalm 142:3-4 we read: *"When my spirit was overwhelmed within me, then Thou knewest my path.*

In the way wherein I walked have they privily laid a snare for me. I looked on my right hand, and beheld, but there was no man that would know me; refuge failed me; no man cared for my soul."

There are times when we all feel like the above — *"no man cared for my soul."* But God knows our path even when our spirit is *"overwhelmed"* within us. The knowledge of God about our suffering is of great comfort to us. II Peter 2;9 says: *"The Lord knoweth how to deliver the godly out of temptations, and to reserve the unjust unto the day of judgment to be punished."* Because of the Lord's knowledge of all things and of our suffering, we can do what I Peter 5:7 says: *"Casting all your care upon Him; for He careth for you."*

3. DIRECTION

We all need direction in our lives. But, where do we get it? To know what to do, where to go, how to do it — these are the common perplexities of our lives. We face questions like these almost every day. Sometimes they loom large in our minds. Should we take that job across the country that promises a higher wage even though it uproots our family? Should we get married to this person even though we have doubts about it? Should we invest in a given project even though there is great risk in the midst of this great potential?

Life is filled with the need for direction. And God knows all about it! Consider the following:

Job 23;10 – *"But He knoweth the way that I take: when He hath tried me, I shall come forth as gold"*

Psalm 1:6 – *"For the Lord knoweth the way of the righteous"*

Psalm 32:8 – *"I will instruct thee and teach thee in the way which thou shalt go: I will guide thee with Mine eye"*

Psalm 37:5 – *"Commit thy way unto the LORD; trust also in Him; and He shall bring it to pass"*

Psalm 37:18 – *"The LORD knoweth the days of the upright: and their inheritance shall be for ever"*

The way we should go is often not observable by us because we do not trust in God's sovereign care and knowledge. If He knows the way, then His way is what we need to follow! Psalm 37:34 says: *"Wait on the LORD, and keep His way."* The way of the Lord is often revealed through His Word. It gives direction to us about many things in our lives. The Lord's vast knowledge of all things allows Him to communicate (in the Bible) eternal principles that govern all decision-making throughout all time. Only an omniscient God could arrange that!

Psalm 119:1 says *"Blessed are the undefiled in the way, who walk in the law of the LORD."* Psalm 119:5 adds: *O that my ways were directed to keep Thy statutes."* Psalm 119:27 states: *"Make me to understand the way of Thy precepts: so shall I talk of Thy wondrous works."* The way we should go is the way of the Lord that is revealed over and over again in His Word. We need to trust the God Who knows the way we should go and what we should do.

4. UNDERSTANDING

We usually fear what we don't understand. We are hesitant to respond or to trust because of it. Fear is the opposite of trust. It is difficult for us to trust something or someone that we do not really understand. God's knowledge is helpful in these cases. He understands everything, and the more we understand and know Him, the more we understand life and ourselves. Proverbs 9:10 makes it clear that *"the knowledge of the Holy One is understanding."*

Hebrews 11:3 says that it is *"Through faith we understand that the worlds were framed by the word of God, so that things which are seen were not made of things which do appear."* Belief is essential to understanding. We must believe God and His word, the Bible, in order to gain understanding of such difficult issues as the origin of the solar system.

Understanding of God's ways with His people Israel has not always been clear. The apostle Paul discussed these problems in some detail in Romans 9-11 and concluded the whole discussion

with these marvelous words about God's
knowledge (Romans 11:33-36):

*" O the depth of the riches both of the
wisdom and knowledge of God! How
unsearchable are His judgments, and
His ways past finding out! For who
hath known the mind of the Lord? Or
who hath been His counselor? Or who
hath first given to Him, and it shall be
recompensed unto him again? For of
Him, and through Him, and to Him, are
all things: to Whom be glory for ever.
Amen."*

Our understanding demands trust in the
God Who knows all things and knows
why they are happening as they are. The
more we know of Him and His ways, the
clearer things become and the more we
understand.

Prayer, suffering, direction, and
understanding – each requires trust in
the infinite wisdom and knowledge of
God. To believe that God does not know
certain things is not only to insult Him,
but it leaves us helpless and hopeless in
these matters of practical concern.
When we observe the greatness of God's
knowledge, it brings out our needs –

needs for honesty, acceptance, and trust. But, there is one more thing!

It reveals the need of THANKSGIVING and PRAISE!

King David declared in Psalm 139:17: *"How precious also are Thy thoughts unto me, O God! How great is the sum of them!"* In speaking of God's great omniscience, David wrote in Psalm 139:6: *"Such knowledge is too wonderful* (too difficult to comprehend) *for me; it is high, I cannot attain unto it."* Did you notice those words – *"precious"* and *"wonderful"*? They are words of praise to God for the knowledge that He has!

Daniel praised the Lord for His knowledge and for the possibilities that were available to him in revealing the dream of Nebuchadnezzar, the King of Babylon. In Daniel 2:19 we read: *"Then Daniel blessed the God of heaven."* He goes on in verses 20-23 to say:

"Blessed be the Name of God for ever and ever: for wisdom and might are His: And He changeth the times and the seasons: He removeth kings, and

setteth up kings: He giveth wisdom unto the wise, and knowledge to them that know understanding: He revealeth the deep and secret things: He knoweth what is in the darkness, and the light dwelleth with Him. I thank Thee, and praise Thee, O Thou God of my fathers, Who hast given me wisdom and might, and hast made known unto me now what we desired of Thee: for Thou hast now made known unto us the king's matter."

Colossians 2:3 says of our Lord Yeshua that in Him *"are hidden all the treasures of wisdom and knowledge."* The Apostle Paul writes in Ephesians 3:17-21 about the love of Messiah and says that if we know it we will discover that it surpasses certain levels of knowledge. He ends the discussion by saying in verses 20-21:

"Now unto Him that is able to do exceeding abundantly above all that we ask or think, according to the power that worketh in us, unto Him be glory in the church by Christ Jesus throughout all ages, world without end. Amen."

Knowing that God knows all things should bring out our praise and thanksgiving to Him. Praise the Lord that He knows everything! Because of Who He is, His vast knowledge is worth trusting at all times – Hallelujah!

Chapter 9
Can We Trust God?

A girl in her twenties was sitting at the counter of a restaurant in Iowa where I stopped for a meal. She looked terrible and had obviously not had a bath or shampoo in weeks. She smelled and her eyes were bloodshot. She asked me for a smoke, which, of course, I did not have. Instead, I asked her where she was from. She said, "Nowhere." Then I asked, "Where are you going?" Again, she said, "Nowhere." I finally asked, "What's wrong?" She turned and looked intently at me and began to cry uncontrollably. Her parents had divorced when she was a young child and she was put into a special institution for girls that nobody wanted. Although her parents were church people and had taken her to Sunday School, they rarely came to see her while she was in that institution. When old enough to be on her own, she hit the streets, wandering from town to town. She had been misused and abused through various sexual encounters and promises. It's an old story, but it still hurts to hear it again. She had lost all confidence in anyone or anything and did not trust me

238

either. As I began to tell her about God's love for her, she asked, "Can He be trusted?" I answered, "Of course. He's God!" She countered, "Why should I trust Him? Everyone else has let me down!"

To make a very long story short, this young woman became a believer in Jesus Christ as Lord and Savior that day. A fine Christian couple took her in and loved her as she had never known before. She learned to trust God and His people who cared for her.

Life is filled with many heartaches and disappointments. God seems so far away, and we often are not sure what He can or will do about it. Can He really be trusted? Upon what evidence do we say that He can?

When a friend lost his job, I watched his trust in God slowly deteriorate. He was losing faith in a God Who cares because He saw little evidence of God's concern. He was out looking for work every day for awhile, but soon gave up. He became depressed and started drinking. The bottle became his relief medicine, and his trust in God was replaced by the

sedative of alcohol. What a tragedy!
Does God care when you lose your job?
Can He be trusted to do something about
it?

THE BASIS OF TRUST

What causes us to trust anyone? When
we are small children, it seems we have
a natural instinct to trust our parents
until their actions or words prove
otherwise. Do we trust people simply
because they are figures of authority?
Do we trust the doctor to whom we must
go for physical help? Do we trust our
political and civic leaders? Do we trust
our pastors? What is the basis of trust?
How does it apply to God?

Three Factors that Build Trust

1. A person must tell the truth.
2. A person must do right and be fair
   or just.
3. A person must be dependable or
   reliable.

These three factors are necessary if real
trust in a person is to exist. It is
interesting that these important

qualities are found in three attributes of God to which the Bible often points us.

1. God is holy – He will not lie to us.
2. God is just – He will always do right.
3. God is faithful – He is always dependable.

GOD IS HOLY!

In some respects, this is the major attribute of God. According to Isaiah 6:3, the angels of God cry: *"Holy, holy, holy is the LORD of hosts. The whole earth is full of His glory!"*

The Hebrew word for "holy" (*kadesh*) and the Greek word (*hagios*) refer to that which is "separate." God is separate in two ways. He is separate from all that He created and He is separate from all that is unclean or sinful. One deals with His greatness or majesty, and the other, His moral purity.

God is separate from His creation!

Psalm 99:2-3 says: *"The LORD is great in Zion; and He is high above all the people. Let them praise Thy great and terrible Name; for it is holy."* His holiness separates Him from His creatures. Psalm 99:5 adds: *"Exalt ye the LORD our God, and worship at His footstool; for He is holy."* Psalm 99:9 says somewhat the same: *"Exalt the LORD, our God, and worship at His holy hill, for the LORD our God is holy."*

Isaiah 57:15 states: *"For thus saith the high and lofty One that inhabiteth eternity, Whose Name is Holy; I dwell in the high and holy place, with him also that is of a contrite and humble spirit, to revive the spirit of the humble, and to revive the heart of the contrite ones."* Again, the emphasis is on His exalted position. He is separate from all His creation. To identify Him with that which He created is the root of idolatry.

Psalm 105:42 speaks of His *"holy promise"* to Abraham and Psalm 98:1 tells us of His *"holy arm"* that has gained Him the victory. Psalm 47:8 tells of His *"holy throne"* from which He reigns over the nations, and Psalm 48:1 speaks of His *"holy mountain,"* Mount Zion, the city of the great King.

Deuteronomy 26:15 says: *"Look down from Thy holy habitation, from heaven, and bless Thy people Israel, and the land which Thou hast given us, as Thou swarest unto our fathers, a land that floweth with milk and honey."*

God is not like us in terms of holiness though we are like Him in terms of personality. He is separate and shall ever remain so. The Creator is not to be confused with, nor lowered to, His creation.

Israel is separate from other nations!

Leviticus 27:28 says: *"Notwithstanding no devoted thing, that a man shall devote unto the LORD of all that he hath, both of man and beast, and of the field of his possession, shall be sold or redeemed: every devoted thing is most holy unto the LORD."*

In addition to the above, certain foods were off limits to the people of Israel. God gave them a special diet to make them "holy" or separate from all the nations around them. It would remind them that they were the Lord's people.

Leviticus 11:44-45 says: *"For I am the LORD your God: ye shall therefore sanctify yourselves, and ye shall be holy; for I am holy: neither shall ye defile yourselves with any manner of creeping thing that creepeth upon the earth. For I am the LORD that bringeth you up out of the land of Egypt, to be your God: ye shall therefore be holy, for I am holy."* Sometimes holiness is defined by that which we do not do.

In Deuteronomy 14:1-2 we read: *"Ye are the children of the LORD your God: ye shall not cut yourselves, nor make any baldness between your eyes for the dead. For thou art an holy people unto the LORD thy God, and the LORD hath chosen thee to be a peculiar people unto Himself, above all the nations that are upon the earth."* Verse 21 adds the point once more: *"for thou art an holy people unto the LORD thy God."* Israel was to be separate from other nations by diet as well as many other practices and observances. Their holiness did not refer in these cases to their moral purity, but to their peculiar practices. They were to be different and separate from the nations around them.

God's creatures are not always reliable, as many of us have frequently found out! People will disappoint you and let you down. That is why God's holiness is so important to understand. He is separate from His creation and unlike it in so many ways!

The Importance of Moral Purity

The major idea people usually have when thinking about holiness is moral purity – being separate from all that is sinful or unclean. That is absolutely essential if God is to be trusted.

Psalm 24:3-4 says: *"Who shall ascend into the hill of the LORD? Or who shall stand in His holy place? He that hath clean hands, and a pure heart; who hath not lifted up his soul unto vanity, nor sworn deceitfully."* Holiness demands *"clean hands and a pure heart."* There can be no deceit or idolatry.

God's holiness means that there is no sin in Him at all. He is incapable of committing a sin and will never do any wrong. Hebrews 6:18 tells us that it is impossible for God to lie! I John 1:5

says: *"God is light and in Him is no darkness at all."*

Because God is holy, He demands holiness in His people. I Peter 1:15-16 states this very clearly: *"But as He which hath called you is holy, so be ye holy in all manner of conversation; Because it is written, Be ye holy; for I am holy."* Hebrews 12:14 tells us to pursue holiness and that without it, we cannot see the Lord as we should!

One of the important Biblical texts dealing with the need of holiness or separation among God's people is found in II Corinthians 6:14-7:1:

"Be ye not unequally yoked together with unbelievers: for what fellowship hath righteousness with unrighteousness? And what communion hath light with darkness? And what concord hath Christ with Belial? Or what part hath he that believeth with an infidel? And what agreement hath the temple of God with idols? For ye are the temple of the living God; as God hath said, I will dwell in them, and walk in them; and I will be their God, and they shall be My

people. Wherefore come out from among them, and be ye separate, saith the Lord, and touch not the unclean thing, and I will receive you, and will be a Father unto you, and ye shall be My sons and daughters, saith the Lord Almighty. Having therefore these promises, dearly beloved, let us cleanse ourselves from all filthiness of the flesh and spirit, perfecting holiness in the fear of God."

Separation from unbelievers is taught in the above passage as well as separation from *"all filthiness of the flesh and spirit."* When we say that God is holy, we mean that He is totally separate from sin in every way. Because of that, we can trust Him.

Psalm 89:34-37 indicates that God's holiness backs up the veracity of His promises:

"My covenant will I not break, nor alter the thing that is gone out of My lips. Once have I sworn by My holiness that I will not lie unto David. His seed shall endure for ever, and his throne as the stars before Me. It shall be established

forever as the moon, and as a faithful witness in heaven."

God swears by the fact of His separateness from all creation and all sin. That means that He will do what He has said. He is absolutely trustworthy because of it!

After I spoke at a Bible conference in the Midwest on the subject of sin and what to do about it, a man approached me with tears in his eyes and asked: "Will God really forgive us for what we have done?" He went on to tell me that as a result of an affair (adultery) he had been filled with guilt and doubts about his salvation. He wanted assurance that God had forgiven him. He asked: "Can adultery be forgiven?" I asked him, "What does the Bible say?" He said, "Well, I know it says that, but how do we know for sure?" I then told him that his problem was in not trusting God to do what He says. I reminded him that He does not lie. If He said He would forgive, then that settles it! We had prayer together, and he confessed to God his reluctance to believe His Word about forgiveness. God's peace filled his heart immediately after his prayer. His problem was centered in his lack of confidence in God. God's holy character guarantees that He is trustworthy – He will not lie to us – Praise the Lord!

GOD IS JUST!

In order to trust someone, you must believe that he or she will do right. Justice and fairness are essential. One high school student I talked with had great difficulty in trusting one of his coaches. The boy's attitude was bad, and he knew it. His coach had made a decision to put him on the bench, believing that this boy was guilty of something he never did. As a result, the boy lost confidence in his coach. He could not be trusted. I tried to explain to him that his coach was only human and thus could make mistakes. That did not seem to help this young athlete. All he saw was the injustice. It was just "not fair."

Life is like that. It reminds me of the importance of justice in the nature of God. Genesis 18:25 says: *"Shall not the Judge of all the earth do right?"*

The Hebrew word for "justice" or "righteousness" (*tsadik*) means "straight." There are no crooked dealings by God – no deviation from what is right to do. He always does right. Therefore, He can be trusted.

The Book of Psalms continually affirms God's righteousness. Psalm 11:7 says: *"For the righteous LORD loveth righteousness; His countenance doth behold the upright."* Psalm 19:8 adds: *"The statutes of the LORD are right, rejoicing the heart."* In one of the Messianic Psalms that is quoted in the New Testament Book of Hebrews, we read in Psalm 45:7: *"Thou lovest righteousness, and hatest wickedness."* Psalm 89:14 says: *"Justice and judgment are the habitation of Thy throne."* Psalm 119:137 declares: *"Righteous art Thou, O LORD, and upright are Thy judgments."* Perhaps one of the greatest statements about the justice of God is Psalm 145:17: *"The LORD is righteous in all His ways, and holy in all His works."* God's holiness and righteousness are blended together in His nature. What wonderful encouragement to our hearts! Jeremiah 50:7 calls the LORD *"the habitation of justice.*" In Ezra's prayer in Ezra 9:15 he states: *"O LORD God of Israel, Thou art righteous."*

Because God is righteous, His promise to Israel was kept in spite of their sin and disobedience. A remnant was spared. God will do right. If He promised something and it was based not on human performance but on His own veracity, then He will and must keep His Word. Psalm 50:6 says: *"the heavens declare His righteousness: for God is Judge Himself."*

God's righteousness guarantees that He will keep His covenant. He will judge those who do wrong. In his prayer to God, Daniel confesses the sin of his people and the righteousness of God in judging them. Daniel 9:14 declares: *"for the LORD our God is righteous in all His works which He doeth: for we obeyed not His voice."*

But, what do we do when things are not right?

People often ask about the justice of God when they see the wickedness of this world. Good people often suffer and wicked people seem to be getting away with their terrible deeds. Where is God in all of this? Can He be trusted to rectify these things?

Romans 12:17-21 gives counsel to all of us concerning our frustrations with the lack of justice and righteousness in this world. When you have been the "victim" of evil deeds and nothing has been done to resolve the matter in a just and righteous way, it is easy to get bitter and discouraged and question whether God can be trusted. Consider carefully what this passage in Romans says:

"Recompense to no man evil for evil. Provide things honest in the sight of all men. If it be possible, as much as lieth in you, live peaceably with all men. Dearly beloved, avenge not yourselves, but rather give place unto wrath: for it is written, Vengeance is Mine; I will repay, saith the Lord. Therefore if thine enemy hunger, feed him; if he thirst, give him drink: for in so doing thou shalt heap coals of fire on his head. Be not overcome of evil, but overcome evil with good."

Never take revenge! God has promised to one day settle all accounts. The Book of Revelation pictures a scene in heaven in the future when the seven last plagues are being executed upon the earth. Believers in heaven are singing the song of Moses and the song of the Lamb. Revelation 15:3-4 records: *"Great and marvelous are Thy works, Lord God Almighty; just and true are Thy ways, Thou King of saints. Who shall not fear Thee, O Lord, and glorify Thy Name? for Thou only art holy: for all nations shall come and worship before Thee; for Thy judgments are made manifest."*

When one of the angels pours out the wrath of God upon planet earth during one of the seven last plagues, we read in Revelation 16:5-6: *"Thou art righteous, O Lord, which art, and wast, and shalt be, because Thou hast judged thus. For they have shed the blood of saints and prophets, and Thou hast given them blood to drink; for they are worthy* (in other words – they deserve it!). *"* In Revelation 16:7 we read: *"Even so, Lord God Almighty, true and righteous are Thy judgments."* Because we can trust God to judge those who do wrong, no one will get away with anything!

His justice means that He will forgive us!

I Peter 3:18 reminds us: *"For Christ also hath once suffered for sins, the just for the unjust, that He might bring us to God, being put to death in the flesh, but quickened by the Spirit."* Romans 3:26 says: *"To declare, I say, at this time His righteousness: that He might be just, and the Justifier of him which believeth in Jesus."*

We rejoice in God's justice and righteousness that causes Him to forgive us for our sins because of our trust in the finished work of His Son, our Savior, our Lord Yeshua, the Messiah of Israel! I John 1:9 says: *"If we confess our sins, He is faithful and just to forgive us our sins, and to cleanse us from all unrighteousness."* What a blessed promise this is to our hearts! God's justice makes our forgiveness possible because Yeshua died in our place – praise the Lord! Therefore, God can be completely trusted – He is just!

He will never forget our work for Him!

God is so trustworthy that we can count on Him to reward whatever we have done for Him. His justice is behind it. Hebrews 6:10 gives us this wonderful encouragement: *"For God is not unrighteous to forget your work and labor of love, which ye have shewed toward His Name, in that ye have ministered to the saints, and do minister."*

Many people do not believe that anyone notices, much less cares, about what they do. But, God, Who is just and righteous, is One Who cares. Nothing escapes His notice. He remembers and He will not forget! I shared with a dear woman whose job was not usually noticed by other people that God would reward her. She washed dishes in the church's kitchen for various dinners and banquets. She had begun to feel that no one really cared about what she was doing. When I shared Hebrews 6:10 with her, her eyes brightened and she said: "Do you mean that God notices my washing these dishes?" I answered, "No doubt about it!" I then said, "And what's more, He will reward you for your faithfulness to Him, even though no one else ever sees what you have done." God cares and will reward us because He is righteous and just!

GOD IS FAITHFUL!

In addition to the fact that He is holy and righteous, our God is faithful. Deuteronomy 7:9 says: *"Know therefore that the LORD thy God, He is God, the faithful God, which keepeth covenant and mercy with them that love Him and keep His commandments to a thousand generations."* Psalm 89:1 speaks of His *"faithfulness to all generations."* Psalm 89:5 adds: *"And the heavens shall praise Thy wonders, O LORD, Thy faithfulness also in the congregation of Thy saints."* And, in verse 8: *"O LORD, God of hosts, Who is a strong LORD like unto Thee? Or to Thy faithfulness round about Thee?"*

Concerning King David, the Lord said in Psalm 89:24: *"But My faithfulness and My mercy shall be with him; and in My Name shall his horn be exalted."* In Psalm 89:33 we read these wonderful words about how He cares for His children: *"Nevertheless My lovingkindness will I not utterly take from him, nor suffer My faithfulness to fail.*"

It is very hard to find faithful friends these days. Every one seems to be doing his or her own thing. Where are your friends when you need them? I asked an elderly woman, crippled by arthritis, what she wanted most. The loneliness of that convalescent hospital was difficult for her. She answered: "A faithful friend!" She continued, "Without the Lord, I don't know what I would do. My friends don't come by much anymore."

Without dependability it is difficult to trust a person. God is dependable. The depth of that fact is rooted in the immutability of His character. He does not change, and His faithfulness is always there.

What God's Faithfulness Means to All Believers!

It is very crucial to our ability to trust God to understand what His faithfulness means to us today. The impact of these great promises in the Bible will affect the way we see things and the way we respond to difficult circumstances. God can be trusted because He is the faithful God!

1. It PROVIDES help in times of temptation!

I Corinthians 10:13 says: *"There hath no temptation taken you but such as is common to man; but God is faithful, who will not suffer you to be tempted above that ye are able; but will with the temptation also make a way to escape, that ye may be able to bear it."*

There are times when we are tempted to such an extent that we wonder if we have the ability to endure. God never puts on us more than we can bear. The reason? He is a faithful God.

In talking with a young college student one day, I discovered that he was involved in sexual sin. He said to me that the temptations he experienced were greater than what he was able to endure. In reality, he was blaming God for putting him in the position where he found himself falling into sin. But the Bible is careful in telling us that God does not tempt any person to sin (James 1:13). Because God is faithful to us, He will never allow the temptations to be greater than what we can bear. That's good news!

2. It PROTECTS us from the evil one!

II Thessalonians 3:1-3 teaches us about God's protection:

"Finally brethren, pray for us, that the word of the Lord may have free course, and be glorified, even as it is with you: And that we may be delivered from unreasonable and wicked men: for all men have not faith. But the Lord is faithful, Who shall stablish you, and keep you from evil (Greek: "evil one").

I John 4:4 tells us *"greater is He that is in you, than he that is in the world."*

There are many *"unreasonable and wicked men"* **in this world who oppose the believer and all that God wants us to do for His glory. God knows the problems that we will all face and He has assured us of His divine protection. The Bible tells us that the fear of man is a** *"snare"* **or a trap. We need to fear only the Lord, and to trust Him to protect us.**

3. It PROMISES us forgiveness and cleansing!

I John 1:9 says: *"If we confess our sins, He is faithful and just to forgive us our sins, and to cleanse us from all unrighteousness."* What a blessed assurance this is to our hearts! God is faithful and therefore must forgive us on the basis of our faith in His Son, our Lord Yeshua (Jesus). The death and resurrection of Jesus Christ are still efficacious today to all who believe. God remains faithful to what His Son has done for us already. Therefore, we can be forgiven and cleansed from our sins if we will confess them to Him. That means we must agree with God as to what He says about them, and not try to defend, excuse, explain, or cover what we have done.

4. It PROCLAIMS security for us in the future!

I Thessalonians 5:23-24 tells us:

"And the very God of peace sanctify you wholly; and I pray God your whole spirit and soul and body be preserved blameless unto the coming of our Lord

Jesus Christ. Faithful is He that calleth you, Who also will do it."

The promise of God's preservation of those who believe in Him is based on His faithfulness. He called us to Himself, and He will see to it that we are safe in His arms forever! Hebrews 10:23 adds: *"Let us hold fast the profession of our faith without wavering; for He is faithful that promised."* Our future is secure because God is faithful. II Timothy 2:13 gives us this remarkable promise: *"If we believe not, yet He abideth faithful: He cannot deny Himself."* Praise the Lord! The assurance that we will one day be with the Lord forever is based on Who God is, and not on our performance!

Chapter 10
Does God really Care?

Rabbi Harold Kushner wrote a best-selling book entitled "WHEN BAD THINGS HAPPEN TO GOOD PEOPLE." He was very concerned about suffering and tragedy and about Who God is and what God can do. On page 134 of his book he wrote:

"I believe in God. But I do not believe the same things about Him that I did years ago, when I was growing up or when I was a theological student. I recognize His limitations. He is limited in what He can do by laws of nature and by the evolution of human nature and human moral freedom. I no longer hold God responsible for illnesses, accidents, and natural disasters, because I realize that I gain little and I lose so much when I blame God for those things. I can worship a God Who hates suffering but cannot eliminate it, more easily than I can worship a God Who chooses to make children suffer and die, for whatever exalted reason. Some years ago, when the 'death of God' theology was a fad, I remember seeing a bumper sticker that read, 'My God is not dead; sorry about yours.' I guess my bumper sticker reads, 'My God is not cruel; sorry about yours.'"

Rabbi Kushner was writing out of personal experience. He lost a son through the illness of progeria. During that time, his soul was deeply stirred as he evaluated God's role in the matter. His sensitivity and understanding are appreciated by all who read his book. But in my mind still lingers the question about his understanding of God. His personal experience had affected his understanding. We must never allow our experiences to govern what the Bible actually teaches concerning the character and actions of God. The God of Rabbi Kushner was limited; the God of the Bible is not. Rabbi Kushner was deeply disturbed about God's failure to solve the problems of human suffering; but, the Bible teaches that God has His reasons and that suffering can be a blessing. Much can be gained and learned through those experiences, and the Bible teaches that ultimately, when Messiah returns, all pain, suffering, sorrow, sickness, and death will be gone forever. Our hope does not lie in this life, but in the life to come!

BUT DOES GOD REALLY CARE?

Does He really care about what we are going through? Are we just a part of His great cosmic plan and the "all things" that God is bringing to a great climax without any assurance of love, understanding, and concern from Him?

The Bible teaches that God is personally concerned about all that transpires in our lives. He really cares. He is a loving and merciful God and understands our weaknesses, limitations and temptations. Furthermore, His strength and power are available to all who call upon Him. He can sustain us in the darkness and the pain, bringing comfort to our hearts when our sorrow seems almost unbearable. God's love is continually presented in the Bible as not only a fact, but a great blessing to all who will trust Him!

While eating in a restaurant, the waitress for the table where we were sitting said that she was having a "rough day." Everything seemed to be going wrong. I asked her if there was anything happening in her life that might be causing her to evaluate that day as being difficult. She then began to tell about the problems she was having. Her husband was divorcing her; he was in love with another woman. Her mother and father were blaming her. Her husband had already moved out of the house and was not providing any financial help for her and her children. She was very discouraged, lonely, bitter, and hostile, and when I began to tell her about the love of God, she looked at me with a cold stare and said: "I don't believe that God really cares about me!" It was obvious, as we continued to talk, that she had reasons for her viewpoint. But what I noticed that day about this waitress, I have seen so many times before. That is, that most people do not know the God of the Bible. They relate to Him only by what people have told them – people who say they believe in Him but do not show any love or care to others. That causes them to question whether God really loves and cares. Perhaps that is a valid comparison, but too much of the time, the people who say they believe in the God of the Bible do not know Him well themselves and, as a result, are poor testimonies for Him. The real questions are: "What does the

Bible say about God? Does He really care?"

THE LOVE OF GOD

No other quality of God's character is so precious to the human soul than that of love. God's love will bring comfort and encouragement to the most depressed heart and discouraged life. God loves us in ways that most of us do not understand or ever appreciate. One of the great texts on the love of God is from I John 4:7-10:

"Beloved, let us love one another: for love is of God; and every one that loveth is born of God, and knoweth God. He that loveth not knoweth not God; for God is love. In this was manifested the love of God toward us, because that God sent His only-begotten Son into the world, that we might live through Him. Herein is love, not that we loved God, but that He loved us, and sent His Son to be the propitiation for our sins. Beloved, if God so loved us, we ought also to love one another."

God is not merely love. When we speak of God's love as an essential part of His nature, it is only one side of the many attributes of God. His love would not be God's love if He were not also a God of holiness and righteousness. His love never overlooks sin but is consistent with all that God is and does. His love does not compromise with sin, nor tolerate it. It is not simply sympathy or sentimentality. According to the above passage, God is love. That means that everything He does and says is bathed with the quality of love. He does not simply react to us apart from His essential loving nature. To say that God does not care about us is to deny Who God really is. According to the above Scripture, our ability to love one another is based upon our personal knowledge of God Himself. It tells us that the greatest demonstration of God's love was sending His Son, our Lord Yeshua, the Messiah of Israel, into the world to die for our sins. According to John 3:16: *"God so loved the world that He gave His only-begotten Son."* Romans 5:8 adds: *"But God commendeth His love toward us, in that while we were yet sinners, Christ died for us."*

God's love cares about us when we do not care anything about Him. God's love is unselfish; He always seeks the benefit of the object of His love. His love is voluntary; He gives to us before we ever give to Him. I John 4:19 says, *"We love Him because He first loved us."* God's love is also an everlasting love. Jeremiah 31:3 speaks powerfully of this fact when it says: *"I have loved thee with an everlasting love; Therefore with lovingkindness I have drawn thee."* I Corinthians 13:8 states the never-ending nature of God's love when it says: *"Love never faileth."* Love is the very essence of God's being.

WHOM DOES GOD LOVE?

The Bible is very clear as to the people toward whom God extends His love and those for whom He has great care and concern.

1. God loves His Son!

The Bible tells us that God loves His only-begotten Son, Yeshua HaMashiach, Jesus the Messiah. In Matthew 3:17, Yeshua is called by His Father — *"My beloved Son."* In John 3:35 it says that *"the Father loves the Son."* In John 17:24, in the great prayer of Yeshua to

His heavenly Father, He says, *"For Thou hast loved Me before the foundation of the world."*

2. God loves those who believe in His Son!

In John 16:27 we read*: "For the Father Himself loveth you, because ye have loved Me, and have believed that I came out from God."* I John 3:1 says: *"Behold, what manner of love the Father hath bestowed upon us, that we should be called the sons of God: therefore the world knoweth us not, because it knew Him not."*

Yes, God loves those who believe in His Son Whom He loves in a special and unique way!

3. God loves the Nation of Israel!

While millions in this world hate the Nation of Israel and Jewish people in particular, God loves them! In Deuteronomy 7:6-9 we read of God's great love for Israel:

"For thou art an holy people unto the LORD thy God: the LORD thy God hath

chosen thee to be a special people unto Himself, above all people that are upon the face of the earth. The LORD did not set His love upon you, nor choose you, because ye were more in number than any people; for ye were the fewest of all people: But because the LORD loved you, and because He would keep the oath which He had sworn unto your fathers, hath the LORD brought you out with a mighty hand, and redeemed you out of the house of bondmen, from the hand of Pharaoh king of Egypt. Know therefore that the LORD thy God, He is God, the faithful God, Which keepeth covenant and mercy with them that love Him and keep His commandments to a thousand generations."

In Jeremiah 31:1 we read: *"At the same time, saith the LORD, will I be the God of all the families of Israel, and they shall be My people."* And then, in verse 3 it says: *"The LORD hath appeared of old unto me, saying, Yea, I have loved thee with an everlasting love: therefore with lovingkindness have I drawn thee."*

4. God loves the entire world!

One of the favorite verses of many believers is John 3:16: *"For God so loved the world, that He gave His only-begotten Son, that whosoever believeth in Him should not perish, but have everlasting life."* Yes, God loves sinners and people who reject Him. Obviously, He loves believers in a special way in comparison with His love for those who reject Him. It is also obvious that He loves His Son, Yeshua the Messiah, in a special sense that separates Him from all those who believe in Him. But, make no mistake about it – God's love reaches out to all. In I John 4:7-8 we are told specifically that *"God is love"* – His love flows out of His very nature. Any real love (in the Biblical understanding of the word) must center itself back, in terms of origin and roots, into the nature and character of God Himself.

There are some believers who argue that John 3:16 is speaking only of believers, not unbelievers. They believe that the word "world" should be interpreted as the "world of those who believe." But, this is not necessary at all. Such limitation upon the love of God is not supported by the Biblical evidence. For example, in I Timothy 4:10 we read that the living God is *"the Savior of all men, specially of those that believe."* Of course, His love is special for the believer, but it is also clear that He loves the unbeliever as well, though hating his rebellion and works of iniquity.

HOW DOES GOD SHOW HIS LOVE?

God's love will reveal itself, and must in order truly to be His love. It will show by what He says and does.

1. God shows His love is impartial by the rain!

Matthew 5:45 states: *"for He maketh His sun to rise on the evil and on the good, and sendeth rain on the just and on the unjust."* This application follows His command to *"Love your enemies."* It gives a basic reason – God is impartial in demonstrating His love for all.

2. God shows His love when He disciplines us!

Hebrews 12:5-6 quotes Proverbs 3:11-12: *"And ye have forgotten the exhortation which speaketh unto you as unto children, My son, despise not thou the chastening of the Lord, nor faint when thou art rebuked of Him: For whom the Lord loveth He chasteneth, and scourgeth every son whom He receiveth."*

God disciplines His children – not to make us miserable or to punish us; He loves us as a father would. He cares what happens to us and does not want us to ruin our lives. He will discipline the believer in order that we may not destroy our testimony, victory, peace or joy. Parents who allow their small children to play in the streets when traffic is heavy, without reminding them of the danger or stopping them when they try to do it, simply do not show love for their children. If you care, you must discipline. You must reprove and correct.

3. God shows His love through the death of His Son, Yeshua!

Romans 5:8 says: *"But God commendeth His love toward us, in that, while we were yet sinners, Christ died for us."* I John 4:9-10 says: *"In this was* manifested the love of God toward us, because that God sent His only-begotten Son into the world, that we might live through Him. Herein is love, not that we loved God, but that He loved us, and sent His Son to be the propitiation for our sins." Ephesians 5:25 adds: "Christ loved the church, and gave Himself for it." The great demonstration that God truly loves us and cares about us is the fact that He sent His Son to die for our sins so that we could live forever with Him.

4. God shows His love by sustaining us in times of trial and suffering!

God sustained the children of Israel during all the time of their wilderness wanderings. It was a great demonstration of God's love that He met their needs, even though they continued to rebel and complain against Him. The Book of Isaiah speaks of this marvelous love of God for His people Israel, by which He sustained them through their journeys (Isaiah 63:7-10):

"I will mention the lovingkindnesses of the LORD, and the praises of the LORD, according to all that the LORD hath bestowed on us, and the great goodness toward the house of Israel, which He hath bestowed on them according to His mercies, and according to the multitude of His lovingkindnesses. For He said, Surely they are My people, children that will not lie: so He was their Savior. In all their affliction He was afflicted, and the Angel of His presence saved them: in His love and in His pity He redeemed them; and He bare them, and carried them all the days of old. But they rebelled, and vexed His Holy Spirit: therefore He was turned to be their enemy, and He fought against them."

It is obvious from these verses that when Israel was afflicted, the Lord also felt that affliction. He truly cared. God cared about the people of Israel when they suffering in Egypt. Exodus 2:23-25 says: *"their cry came up unto God by reason of the bondage. And God heard their groaning, and God remembered His covenant with Abraham, with Isaac, and with Jacob. And God looked upon the children of Israel, and God had respect unto them.* " Judges 10:16 says of our Lord's love for Israel: *"and His soul was grieved for the misery of Israel."*

5. God shows His love by being patient with us!

I Corinthians 13:4 says: *"Charity suffereth long"* or "Love is patient." Longsuffering, or patience, is from a Greek word that means "taking a long time to boil." It is always used in respect to persons, not objects or difficult situations. There is another Greek word that translates into English as "patience" and refers to things or circumstances that we have to endure. God is never said to be patient toward things or circumstances. He does not need that kind of patience for He is controlling all things. However, the Bible does say that God is patient or longsuffering toward people.

It is not natural for us to exhibit this longsuffering or patience; it comes from God and is a part of the *"fruit of the Holy Spirit* (Galatians 5:22-23)." It is normal to be quite impatient with the way people act and respond.

I found myself quite upset one day with the way a certain person was doing a job I had asked him to do. I was very impatient with him because the speed with which he was doing this task was not the speed I was demanding. I felt sick inside when I realized that my impatience was getting the best of me. When I sought God's help and confessed my sin, I noticed an immediate change in my attitude. The speed of that person no longer mattered; I was now happy that he was involved in helping me. After all, that is what really counts. I am so glad that God is patient toward us!

God had patience while Noah was building the ark (I Peter 3:20). That generation of people deserved the judgment of God, but God was patient and gave them much opportunity to repent. After 120 years of preaching by Noah, God brought His judgment in the form of a global deluge (flood) upon the earth. Genesis 6:3 reminds us: *"My Spirit shall not always strive with man, for that he also is flesh."* God has great patience toward unbelievers as well as believers. He endures the wickedness and rebellion of unbelievers (Romans

9:22; I Peter 3:20), and He also endures the unfaithfulness and sin of believers. The words *"slow to anger"* in many Old Testament passages are translated into the Greek word for *"longsuffering."* God's patience is often connected with His forgiveness. Exodus 34:6-7 clearly shows that God is *"longsuffering"* and also *"forgiving."*

Our patience is usually tested when we run into unresponsive people. I remember well my lack of patience in dealing with a man who continued to fall back into certain habits of sinning. Over and over again, he would seem to repent, get right with God, and then go back to sinning again. It was one discouraging cycle of events! I thought I loved him and wanted to help, but I found myself becoming more and more impatient with his sinful ways and weaknesses. I know he had a problem, but so did I! I see my problem in better focus when I think of the patience of our Lord. No matter how many times we have fallen, He is there to forgive and pick up the broken pieces. How I praise Him for His loving patience with me!

Yes, God really cares about us! His love constantly demonstrates that care. The Bible is filled with passages that teach of God's love for us. Until we really understand the dimensions of that love, the extent of that love, and the demonstration of that love, we will continue to doubt and question whether or not the God Who made us cares about what we are experiencing. The more we learn, the greater comfort we have. The more we understand, the greater our assurance that He truly cares!

THE MERCY OF GOD

When we speak of mercy, we are talking about the demonstration of God's love in terms of holding back from us what we really deserve. We deserve judgment and hell because of what we have thought, said, and done. But God is a God of mercy; His love makes it possible for us to be protected from the judgment we deserve. One of the great ways I feel loved and cared for by God is when I think of His mercy toward me. Deuteronomy 4:31 says: *"For the LORD thy God is a merciful God; He will not forsake thee, neither destroy thee, nor forget the covenant of thy fathers which*

279

He sware unto them." II Corinthians 1:3 calls Him the *"Father of mercies."* Micah 7:18 says: *"He delighteth in mercy."*

There are two major Hebrew words that are translated with the English word "mercy." The word *rachamim* and the word *chesed* are both found in Psalm 103:4: *"Who crowneth thee with lovingkindness and tender mercies."*

HOW GREAT IS GOD'S MERCY?

Love describes God's character — what God is; mercy describes God's actions — what God does. In I Chronicles 21:13, David said: *"I am in a great strait: let me fall now into the hand of the LORD; for very great are His mercies: but let me not fall into the hand of man."* David was very conscious of the mercy of God and how wonderful and vast it truly is. In Psalm 57:10 we read: *"For Thy mercy is great unto the heavens, and Thy truth unto the clouds."*

Psalm 86:5 tells us: *"For Thou, Lord, art good, and ready to forgive; and plenteous in mercy unto all them that call upon Thee."* Psalm 89:2 adds:

"Mercy shall be built up for ever: Thy faithfulness shalt Thou establish in the very heavens." Psalm 103:8 states: *"The LORD is merciful and gracious, slow to anger, and plenteous in mercy."* Psalm 108:4 continues: *"For Thy mercy is great above the heavens: and Thy truth reacheth unto the clouds."* Psalm 119:64 makes this claim: *"The earth, O LORD, is full of Thy mercy."* Psalm 136 says repeatedly *"His mercy endureth for ever (says it 26 times)."* Mercy extends God's love to us in a special way because it holds back from us what we really deserve. Mercy understands our weaknesses, limitations, and sins, and is a demonstration that God truly cares.

HOW DOES GOD SHOW HIS MERCY TO US?

1. God shows mercy to us by not giving us what we deserve!

If God gave us what we deserve, we would all be in Hell! Lamentations 3:22-23 says: *"It is of the LORD's mercies that we are not consumed, because His compassions fail not. They are new every morning: great is Thy faithfulness."* Thank the Lord that He holds back from us the judgment we deserve – because He is a merciful God! Ephesians 2:1-4 says: *"And you hath He quickened, who were dead in trespasses and sins; wherein in time past ye walked according to the course of this world, according to the prince of the power of the air, the spirit that now worketh in the children of disobedience: Among whom also we all had our conversation in times past in the lusts of our flesh, fulfilling the desires of the flesh and of the mind; and were by nature the children of wrath, even as others. But God, Who is rich in mercy, for His great love wherewith He loved us."* The words *"But God"* show us that there is an answer to the sinful condition of our hearts that lies in the character of God Himself. Because He is *"rich in mercy"* He extends salvation to us, even though we deserve the wrath of God!

2. God shows mercy to us by providing for our needs when we really do not deserve it!

In Nehemiah, we have a great text demonstrating God's care for the children of Israel during their wilderness wanderings – in spite of their rebellion against Him. This text in Nehemiah 9:16-21 speaks eloquently of the mercy of God.

"But they and our fathers dealt proudly, and hardened their necks, and hearkened not to Thy commandments, and refused to obey, neither were mindful of Thy wonders that Thou didst among them; but hardened their necks, and in their rebellion appointed a captain to return to their bondage: but Thou are a God ready to pardon, gracious and merciful, slow to anger, and of great kindness, and forsakest them not. Yea, when they had made them a molten calf, and said, This is thy God that brought thee up out of Egypt, and had wrought great provocations; Yet Thou in Thy manifold mercies forsookest them not in the wilderness: the pillar of the cloud departed not from them by day, to lead them in the way; neither the pillar of fire by night, to shew them light, and the way wherein they should go. Thou gavest also Thy good spirit to instruct them, and withheldest not Thy manna from their mouth, and gavest them water for their thirst. Yea, forty years didst Thou

sustain them in the wilderness, so that they lacked nothing; their clothes waxed not old, and their feet swelled not."

It was the merciful God Who made the difference because of Who He is. Were it not for His mercies, their needs would never have been met. God led them and guided them because He is a merciful God. He gave them food to eat and water to drink because He is merciful. He sustained them. Psalm 145:9 says, *"The LORD is good to all: and His tender mercies are over all His works."*

3. God shows His mercy by forgiving us of our sins!

One of the great evidences of God's tender mercies toward us is the matter of our forgiveness. He forgives all our iniquities and crowns us *"with lovingkindness and tender mercies (Psalm 103:4)."* Psalm 103:8 adds: *"The LORD is merciful and gracious, slow to anger, and plenteous in mercy."* Verse 11 says that His mercy is great.

We have done nothing to deserve it or earn what God offers. It is His mercy that makes our forgiveness possible.

In Psalm 51:1 we have David's words of repentance over his sin with Bathsheba and her husband whom he had killed. He prays: *"Have mercy upon me, O God, according to Thy lovingkindness: according to the multitude of Thy tender mercies blot out my transgression."* David understood that there is no forgiveness apart from the mercies of God. Were it not for His mercy, we would all perish in our sins!

God's mercies become a powerful motivation for serving the Lord. In Romans 12:1 we read: *"I beseech you therefore, brethren, by the mercies of God, that ye present your bodies a living sacrifice, holy, acceptable unto God, which is your reasonable service."* When we remember how wonderful His mercies are, we are motivated to serve Him faithfully.

Some of us try to cover up our sins instead of confessing them to a merciful God Who will forgive us. Proverbs 28:13 says: *"He that covereth his sins shall not prosper: but whoso confesseth and forsaketh them shall have mercy."*

It is possible that one of the reasons why people do not feel that God loves them and cares for them is that sin may be in their minds, hearts, or lifestyles. Sin blinds us to the love and mercy of God. It is the very mercy of God that does not punish us immediately for what we have done. It is the love and mercy of God that grants forgiveness to all who confess and forsake their sin.

SO, DOES GOD REALLY CARE?

How could we ever doubt the loving care of God if we truly believe the Bible? I Peter 5:7 tells us: *"Casting all your care upon Him; for He careth for you."*

One of the greatest messages on the loving care of our God was given by our Lord Yeshua in Matthew 6:25-34. May God encourage our hearts!

"Therefore I say unto you, Take no thought for your life, what ye shall eat, or what ye shall drink; nor yet for your body, what ye shall put on. Is not the life more than meat, and the body than

raiment? Behold the fowls of the air: for they sow not, neither do they reap, nor gather into barns; yet your heavenly Father feedeth them. Are ye not much better than they? Which of you by taking thought can add one cubit unto his stature? And why take ye thought for raiment? Consider the lilies of the field, how they grow; they toil not, neither do they spin: And yet I say unto you, That even Solomon in all his glory was not arrayed like one of these. Wherefore, if God so clothe the grass of the field, which today is, and tomorrow is cast into the oven, shall He not much more clothe you, O ye of little faith? Therefore take no thought, saying, What shall we eat? Or, What shall we drink? Or, Wherewithal shall we be clothed? For after all these things do the Gentiles seek: for your heavenly Father knoweth that ye have need of all these things. But seek ye the kingdom of God, and His righteousness; and all these things shall be added unto you. Take therefore no thought for the morrow: for the morrow shall take thought for the things of itself. Sufficient unto the day is the evil thereof."

This passage teaches that God cares about birds and flowers as well as about the believer. He knows the sparrow that falls from the tree and numbers every hair on our heads. He knows about our hurts and disappointments and cares about the tears that we have shed. He is the great Burden-bearer Who invites us to come to Him because He does care. Hebrews 4:15-16 puts it this way:

"For we have not an high priest which cannot be touched with the feeling of our infirmities; but was in all points tempted like as we are, yet without sin. Let us therefore come boldly unto the throne of grace, that we may obtain mercy, and find grace to help in time of need."

Chapter 11
What is God's Name?

The Hebrew word for the "Name" of God is in the singular — *"shem,"* never used in the plural in reference to God. Also, the Greek word for "name" is the word *"onoma"* which also is only used in its singular form when referring to God. Even Matthew 28:19 which mentions all three Persons of the Godhead still uses the singular form of the word *"name"* when referring to God. His Name is really not a title, but rather refers to His attributes and abilities.

A very important passage related to the identification of God's Name is found in Exodus 3:13-15:

"And Moses said unto God, Behold, when I come unto the children of Israel, and shall say unto them, The God of your fathers hath sent me unto you; and they shall say to me, What is His Name? What shall I say unto them? And God said unto Moses, I AM THAT I AM: and He said, Thus shalt thou say unto the children of Israel, I AM hath sent me unto you. And God said moreover unto Moses, Thus shalt thou

say unto the children of Israel, The LORD God of your fathers, the God of Abraham, the God of Isaac, and the God of Jacob, hath sent me unto you: this is My Name for ever, and this is My memorial unto all generations."

USAGE OF WORDS

In the Hebrew Bible (Old Testament) the word *"God"* appears as a singular word – *El* – 1007 times! This is no small subject! The word *"God"* also appears as a plural word – *Elohim* – and is found 2605 times! The word *Eloah* is used 56 times; the word *Elyon* (*"Most High"*) is found 78 times.

If one is looking up the Biblical facts concerning the usage of the word *"God"* he must examine 3746 occurrences of the word!

But, this is only the beginning! The English word *"LORD"* (all capitals in the King James Version of the Bible) and the word *"Lord"* (capital "L" with small letters following) are found more times than the word translated *"God"*! The Hebrew words *Adown* or *Adonai* are referring to an earthly lord (which, of course, our God is as well!) and they are found 331 times. But, the primary word translated by the capital letters – "LORD" – is what we call the Tetragrammaton – the sacred four letters that Jewish people do not pronounce or write. We have the word *"Yah"* (meaning – LORD) used 52 times, but the word *"Yahveh"* (LORD) is used 6823 times! That is remarkable to say the least! These four letters (English = YHVH) have no consonants so we really do not know how to pronounce the word correctly.

What we do know grammatically about these four letters is that they are rooted in the verb *"to be."* For example, the word *hayah* which means *"was"* refers to the past; the word *hoveh* or *"is"* refers to the present; and the word *yihyeh* or *"will be"* refers to the future. God is described as the One Who is past, present, and future – He exists in all phases of time (which He created) at any one moment of time! It is interesting to notice the references in Revelation 1:5 and 1:8 in the New Testament which speak of Him as the One *"which is, and which was, and which is to come."* Psalm 90:2 says: *"Before the mountains were brought forth, or ever Thou hadst formed the earth and the world, even from everlasting to everlasting, Thou art God."*

To Abraham He said in Genesis 17:1: *"I am the Almighty God."* The Hebrew words are *El Shaddai.*

In trying to understand the usage and meaning of God's Name, we discover a multitude of usages that tell us of His attributes and abilities.

1. His Name refers to His <u>PROVISION</u>!

One of the comforting facts about God is that He is the One Who supplies all of our needs as Philippians 4:19 states: *"But my God shall supply all your need according to His riches in glory by Christ Jesus."*

In Genesis 22:13-14 we have the story of Abraham offering his son, Isaac, upon the altar of sacrifice.

"And Abraham lifted up his eyes, and looked, and behold behind him a ram caught in a thicket by his horns: and

Abraham went and took the ram, and offered him up for a burnt offering in the stead of his son. And Abraham called the name of that place Jehovah-jireh: as it is said to this day, In the mount of the LORD it shall be seen."

The English word *"Jehovah"* that is used to translate the Tetragrammaton actually comes from the Latin. More correctly it should be *Yahveh yireh* – the LORD provides! Back in Genesis 22:8 Abraham said to Isaac: *"My son, God will provide Himself a lamb for a burnt offering."*

In Psalm 23:1, a verse that has comforted many people throughout history, we read: *"The LORD is my Shepherd; I shall not want."* Here we learn that the Name of our Lord is *Yahveh ro'i* – the Shepherd Who provides what we need!

2. His Name refers to His <u>PRESENCE</u>!

One of the comforting facts about the Name of our God is what we read in the last verse of Ezekiel's prophecy when he says (48:35): *"The LORD is there."*

Again, we learn more about the sacred Name of our God – He is *Yahveh shammah.*

3. His Name refers to His <u>PEACE</u>!

What a blessing to know that He is in His character and attributes – PEACE! Judges 6:24 says: *"Then Gideon built an altar there unto the LORD, and called it Jehovah-shalom: unto this day it is yet in Ophrah of the Abiezrites."* Gideon's response was based on what the *"Angel of the LORD"* had revealed to him. In Judges 6:22 we read *"And when Gideon perceived that he was an angel of the LORD, Gideon said, Alas, O Lord GOD! for because I have seen an angel of the LORD face to face."* And then the LORD (*Yahveh*) Himself says: *"Peace be unto thee; fear not: thou shalt not die."* It was then that Gideon worshipped the Lord by building an altar and calling it *Yahveh-shalom* – "The LORD is peace."

4. His Name refers to His <u>POSITION</u>!

The Hebrew words *Yahveh Elyon* are usually translated *"The LORD Most High."* Here are a few examples:

Psalm 7:17 – *"I will praise the LORD according to His righteousness: and will sing praise to the Name of the LORD Most High."*

Psalm 47:2 – *"For the LORD Most High is terrible; He is a great King over all the earth."*

Psalm 83:18 – *"That men may know that Thou, Whose Name alone is JEHOVAH* (Yahveh), *art the Most High over all the earth."*

Psalm 92:8 – *"But Thou, LORD, art Most High for evermore."*

We are told about His exalted position in Psalm 8:1 where we read: *"O LORD our Lord, how excellent is Thy Name in all the earth! Who has set Thy glory above the heavens."* The *"heavens"* are certainly spectacular demonstrations of the power and greatness of our God. But, His glory is *"<u>above</u> the heavens."*

Psalm 148:13 adds: *"Let them praise the Name of the LORD: for His Name alone is excellent; His glory is above the earth and heaven."*

It is fascinating to observe the name of the major airline of the Nation of Israel. It is called *EL AL* – which means "GOD MOST HIGH."

5. His Name refers to His <u>PERFECTION</u>!

The Bible speaks of our LORD as *"The LORD our righteousness."* The Hebrew words are *Yahveh tzidkenu.* In Jeremiah 23:5-6 we read these wonderful words about our Messiah: *"Behold, the days come, saith the LORD, that I will raise unto David a righteous Branch, and a King shall reign and prosper, and shall execute judgment and justice in the earth. In His days Judah shall be saved, and Israel shall dwell safely: and this is His Name whereby He shall be called, THE LORD OUR RIGHTEOUSNESS."*

Jeremiah 33:15-16 also says: *"In those days, and at that time, will I cause the Branch of righteousness to grow up unto David; and He shall execute judgment and righteousness in the land. In those days shall Judah be saved, and Jerusalem shall dwell safely: and this is the Name wherewith she shall be called, The LORD our righteousness."*

6. His Name refers to His <u>PEOPLE</u> Whom He sanctifies!

When we read of the LORD sanctifying His people it refers to the fact of how He separates them from the nations around them. In the instructions which the LORD gave to the children of Israel concerning the Shabat (Sabbath days), it is clear that these regulations were designed only for the children of Israel and not for any Gentiles. It is the covenant sign between the LORD and His people for the covenant of Moses. Exodus 31:13 says:

"Speak thou also unto the children of Israel, saying, Verily My Sabbaths ye shall keep: for it is a sign between Me and you throughout your generations; that ye may know that I am the LORD that doth sanctify you."

That last phrase contains the Hebrew words *Yahveh mekadishkhem.*

We also have the words of Leviticus 19:2: *"Speak unto all the congregations of the children of Israel, and say unto them, Ye shall be holy: for I the LORD your God am holy."* Holiness as we have learned previously in our study refers to how God is separate from the physical and material creation which He has made as well as being separate from sin. God's people are to be sanctified or holy, separate from sin but also separate from the nations surrounding them. Deuteronomy 7:6 says *"For thou art an holy people unto the LORD thy God: the LORD thy God hath chosen thee to be a special people unto Himself, above all people that are upon the face of the earth."*

One of the ways in which the LORD separated His people was by giving them a special diet with many restrictions as to what they were to eat or not eat. In Leviticus 11:44-45 we read:

"For I am the LORD your God: ye shall therefore sanctify yourselves, and ye shall be holy; for I am holy: neither

298

shall ye defile yourselves with any manner of creeping thing that creepeth upon the earth. For I am the LORD that bringeth you up out of the land of Egypt, to be your God: ye shall therefore be holy, for I am holy."

Similar instructions about their diet were given in Deuteronomy 14. In verse two it says: *"For thou art an holy people unto the LORD thy God, and the LORD hath chosen thee to be a peculiar people unto Himself, above all the nations that are upon the earth."*

Many Jewish people want to blend in with the Gentiles around them, and so they avoid the kosher diet and eat whatever the Gentiles eat. This was not the will of the LORD for the children of Israel. They were to be *"holy"* or separate from the nations. After describing what they could eat or not eat, we read in the last part of Deuteronomy 14:21 these words: *"for thou art an holy people unto the LORD thy God."*

Leviticus 20:7-8 says: *"Sanctify yourselves therefore, and be ye holy: for I am the LORD your God. And ye shall keep My statutes, and do them: I am the LORD which sanctify you."*

Leviticus 21:8 has some special instructions for the priests, the sons of Aaron. We read these reads: *"Thou shalt sanctify him therefore; for he offereth the bread of thy God: he shall be holy unto thee: for I the LORD, which sanctify you, am holy."* Those last words about the LORD sanctifying His people are repeated in Leviticus 21:15, 23 and in 22:9, 16.

The word for *"Holy One"* is the Hebrew *kadosh.* Isaiah uses it to describe our God 29 times. Isaiah 40:25 states: *"To whom then will ye liken Me, or shall I be equal? saith the Holy One."* Isaiah 43:3 says: *"For I am the LORD thy God, the Holy One of Israel, thy Savior."*

7. His Name refers to His <u>POWER</u>!

Our God is powerful as we have already learned in our study of His nature, attributes, and abilities. But, His Name reveals His power.

In Genesis 17:1 we read: *"And when Abram was ninety years old and nine, the LORD appeared to Abram, and said unto him, I am the Almighty God; walk before Me, and be thou perfect."* The words *"Almighty God"* are the translated of the Hebrew words *El Shaddai* – "the God of power or strength."

God has the power to heal. Exodus 15:26 says: *"I will put none of these diseases upon thee, which I have brought upon the Egyptians: for I am the LORD that healeth thee."* He is *Yahveh rophe.* It involves physical healing but also spiritual and emotional healing as well.

God is also *Yahveh Sabaoth* – "the LORD of hosts." He is the Commander of the army of angels who are at His bidding. Psalm 46:7 says: *"The LORD of hosts is with us; the God of Jacob is our refuge."* Isaiah 1:24 adds: *"Therefore saith the Lord, the LORD of hosts, the mighty One of Israel..."*

The Bible uses the Hebrew word *abhir* and translates *"Mighty One"* which means "to be strong." It is used in Deuteronomy 10:17 when it says: *"For the LORD your God is God of gods, and*

*Lord of lords, a great God, a mighty,
and a terrible, which regardeth not
persons, nor taketh reward."* He is
called *"the mighty God of Jacob"* in
Psalm 132:3, 5 and Isaiah 49:26.

There are two basic facts about the
power of God that we must understand if
we are to know the God of the Bible.

1. God's power is unique!

What that means simply is that no one
can do what God can do! This is evident
in creation as well as in His control of
time and events. Consider this amazing
passage in Isaiah 44:6-8:

*"Thus saith the LORD (Yahveh) the
King of Israel, and His Redeemer the
LORD (Yahveh Sabaoth) of hosts; I am
the first, and I am the last; and beside
Me there is no God. And who, as I, shall
call, and shall declare it, and set it in
order for Me, since I appointed the
ancient people? And the things that are
coming, and shall come, let them shew
unto them. Fear ye not, neither be
afraid: have not I told thee from that
time, and have declared it? ye are even
My witnesses. Is there a God beside*

Me? Yea, there is no God; I know not any."

2. God's power is unlimited!

This simply means that there is nothing too hard for Him to do! Psalm 145:3 says *"Great is the LORD, and greatly to be praised; and His greatness is unsearchable."* Verses 10 and 11 say: *"All Thy works shall praise Thee, O LORD; and Thy saints shall bless Thee. They shall speak of the glory of Thy kingdom, and talk of Thy power."* Genesis 18:14 reminds us: *"Is any thing too hard for the LORD?"* The answer of the Bible is clear – He can do anything He wants to do – there is no limit to His power!

WHAT DOES THE NEW TESTAMENT TEACH ABOUT THE NAME OF GOD?

The New Testament uses the Greek word *kurios* 600 times! This Greek word is the only word used in the Greek translation of the Old Testament to translate the Tetragrammaton – the word "LORD" or *Yahveh*.

We also have the Greek word *despotes* used five times. It refers to a sovereign ruler. The word *theos* is translated *"God"* over 1000 times in the New Testament. The word *theotes* meaning "Godhead" is used twice in Colossians 2:9 and Romans 1:20.

HOW SHOULD WE RESPOND TO THE NAME OF THE LORD GOD?

This is a very important question and one which is not often considered in discussions about the Bible's teaching about God. The are at least seven basic responses that we should have toward the sacred NAME of God.

1. We should FEAR His Name!

This generation manifests very little genuine fear of God. We are warned not to fear man – that is a "snare" or a "trap." Yeshua told us not to fear the one who can only kill the body, but rather fear the One Who can cast both body and soul into hell!

Proverbs 1:28-33 is a very important passage dealing with the fear of God:

"Then shall they call upon Me, but I will not answer; they shall seek Me early, but they shall not find Me: For that they hated knowledge, and did not choose the fear of the LORD: They would none of My counsel: they despised all My reproof. Therefore shall they eat of the fruit of their own way, and be filled with their own devices. For the turning away of the simple shall slay them, and the prosperity of fools shall destroy them. But whoso hearkeneth unto Me shall dwell safely, and shall be quiet from fear of evil."

The basic human problem? They *"did not choose the fear of the LORD."* Proverbs 1:7 says *"The fear of the LORD is the beginning of knowledge: but fools despise wisdom and instruction."* Proverbs 9:10 continues: *"The fear of the LORD is the beginning of wisdom: and the knowledge of the Holy (One) is understanding."* Proverbs 8:13 says that *"the fear of the LORD is to hate evil: pride, and arrogancy, and the evil way, and the forward mouth, do I hate."* Proverbs 14:26 says that *"In the fear of the LORD is strong confidence: and His children shall have a place of refuge."*

Proverbs 16:6 tells us that *"by the fear of the LORD men depart from evil."*

2. We should PRAISE His Name!

Psalm 113:1-3 puts it clearly: *"Praise ye the LORD. Praise, O ye servants of the LORD, praise the Name of the LORD. Blessed be the Name of the LORD from this time forth and forevermore. From the rising of the sun unto the going down of the same the LORD's Name is to be praised."* Psalm 9:2 says: *"I will sing praise to Thy Name, O Thou Most High."* Psalm 44:8 states: *"In God we boast all the day long, and praise Thy Name forever."* Psalm 54:6 adds: *"I will praise Thy Name, O LORD; for it is good."* Psalm 69:30 says: *"I will praise the Name of God with a song, and will magnify Him with thanksgiving."*

3. We should GLORIFY His Name!

Psalm 29:2 says: *"Give unto the LORD the glory due unto his Name; worship the LORD in the beauty of holiness."* All nations are told to glorify His Name in Psalm 86:9: *"All nations whom Thou hast made shall come and worship before Thee, O Lord: and shall glorify*

Thy Name." **Verse 12 of Psalm 86 adds:**
"I will praise Thee, O Lord my God; with all my heart: and I will glorify Thy Name for evermore."

Psalm 115:1 warns us about glorifying ourselves: *"Not unto us, O LORD, not unto us, but unto Thy Name give glory, for Thy mercy, and for Thy truth's sake."*

4. We should <u>TRUST</u> His Name!

Psalm 33:21 says: *"For our heart shall rejoice in Him, because we have trusted in His holy Name."* **Psalm 52:7-9 speaks of our need of trusting in the Lord and not in what we have:** *"Lo, this is the man that made not God his strength; but trusted in the abundance of his riches, and strengthened himself in his wickedness. But I am like a green olive tree in the house of God: I trust in the mercy of God for ever and ever. I will praise Thee for ever, because Thou hast done it: and I will wait on Thy Name; for it is good before Thy saints."*

In Psalm 61:1-4 King David speaks of the need to trust in the Lord:

"Hear my cry, O God; attend unto my prayer. From the end of the earth will I cry unto Thee, when my heart is overwhelmed: lead me to the rock that is higher than I. For Thou hast been a Shelter for me, and a strong Tower from the enemy. I will abide in Thy tabernacle for ever: I will trust in the covert of Thy wings."

Psalm 62:8 tells us: *"Trust in Him at all times; ye people, pour out your heart before Him: God is a Refuge for us."* The Psalmist writes in Psalm 73:28: *"But it is good for me to draw near to God: I have put my trust in the Lord GOD, that I may declare all Thy works."*

5. We should <u>CALL UPON</u> His Name!

The principle before us is one of complete dependency upon the LORD! Psalm 18:1-6 makes it clear:

"I will love Thee, O LORD, my strength. The LORD is my Rock, and my Fortress, my Strength, in Whom I will trust; my Buckler, and the Horn of my salvation, and my high Tower. I will call upon the LORD, Who is worthy to be praised: so

shall I be saved from mine enemies. The sorrow of death compassed me, and the floods of ungodly men made me afraid. The sorrow of hell compassed me about: the snares of death prevented me. In my distress I called upon the LORD, and cried unto my God: He heard my voice out of His temple, and my cry came before Him, even into His ears."

What a blessing to know that God hears us when we cry to Him and call upon His Name! Psalm 105:1 admonishes us: *"O give thanks unto the LORD; call upon His Name."* Psalm 116:1-4 reminds us to call upon His Name – *"I love the LORD, because He hath heard my voice and my supplications. Because He hath inclined His ear unto me, therefore will I call upon Him as long as I live. The sorrows of death compassed me, and the pains of hell gat hold upon me: I found trouble and sorrow. Then called I upon the Name of the LORD: O LORD, I beseech Thee, deliver my soul."*

God has promised to hear the cries of His children when we call upon His Name. Psalm 145:18 says: *"The LORD is nigh* (near) *unto all them that call upon Him, to all that call upon Him in truth."*

A wonderful passage that exhorts us to call upon the Name of the LORD is found in Isaiah 55:6-9:

"Seek ye the LORD while He may be found, call ye upon Him while He is near: Let the wicked forsake his way, and the unrighteous man his thoughts: and let him return unto the LORD, and He will have mercy upon him; and to our God, for He will abundantly pardon. For My thoughts are not your thoughts, neither are your ways My ways, saith the LORD. For as the heavens are higher than the earth, so are My ways higher than your ways, and My thoughts than your thoughts."

We are exhorted to call upon the LORD because His ways and His thoughts are greater than anything we could come up with to solve our problems! He will pardon and forgive when we turn unto the LORD! Praise the Lord!

6. We should BELIEVE in His Name!

John 1:12 says: *"But as many as received Him* (our Lord Yeshua)*, to them gave He power to become the sons* *of God, even to them that believe on His Name."* His Name is not simply a title – it refers to His true identity, His attributes and abilities.

John 3:16-18 says: *"For God so loved the world, that He gave His only-begotten Son, that whosoever believeth in Him should not perish, but have everlasting life. For God sent not His Son into the world to condemn the world; but that the world through Him might be saved. He that believeth on Him is not condemned: but he that believeth not is condemned already, because he hath not believed in the Name of the only-begotten Son of God."*

The words *"only-begotten"* are used five times by the Apostle John and once by the writer of Hebrews in Hebrews 11:17 when he refers to Abraham's son Isaac as his *"only-begotten"* son. Abraham had other children, but Isaac was the unique son through whom the Messiah would come. Yeshua is the "one and only," the absolutely unique Son of God! We must believe on the Name of the Son of God in order to be saved and have eternal life!

7. We must CONFESS His Name!

The issue here is loyalty. It means more than just saying the words that you believe in Yeshua! Consider carefully the contrast that is presented in Matthew 10:32-33:

"Whosoever therefore shall confess Me before men, him will I confess also before My Father which is in heaven. But whosoever shall deny Me before men, him will I also deny before My Father which is in heaven."

The opposite of confession is denial! I John 2:22-23 contain similar words: *"Who is a liar but he that denieth that Jesus* (Yeshua) *is the Christ* (Messiah)*? He is antichrist, that denieth the Father and the Son. Whosoever denieth the Son, the same hath not the Father: but he that acknowledgeth* (confesses) *the Son hath the Father also."*

Romans 10:9-10 makes it clear that confession of His true character and identity is essential to our salvation:

"That if thou shalt confess with thy mouth the Lord Jesus (Yeshua)*, and*

shalt believe in thine heart that God hath raised Him from the dead, thou shalt be saved. For with the heart man believeth unto righteousness; and with the mouth confession is made unto salvation."

Philippians 2:9-11 expresses it in powerful terms:

"Wherefore God also hath highly exalted Him, and given Him a Name which is above every name: That at the Name of Jesus (Yeshua) *every knee should bow, of things in heaven, and things in earth, and things under the earth; and that every tongue should confess that Jesus Christ* (Yeshua HaMashiach) *is Lord, to the glory of God the Father."*

The only proper response to all of this is to say "AMEN" and "PRAISE THE LORD" and "GLORY TO GOD!"

Chapter 12
How Do We Please God?

The focus today is man, not God. That's
our problem! The Bible teaches that we
were not designed to please ourselves.
We were created to glorify the God Who
made us. What does God want us to do?
He wants us to honor and praise Him in
all we think, say, and do. We need to get
our eyes off of ourselves and on to the
plan and purpose of God. The peace,
joy, love, and purpose in life that all of
us desire are to be found in the pursuit
of God, not in self-enhancement or self-
aggrandizement.

But, that raises some questions. How do
we please God? What can we do to
change the focus of our lives from
ourselves to the God Who made us?
What are we doing now that hinders our
ability to please Him? What differences
can we expect to find once we start
trying to please God?

WHY SHOULD WE PLEASE GOD?

That's a good question! Our natural
tendency is to please ourselves. It is a
part of what the Apostle Paul called the

"carnal mind." He said the following in Romans 8:6-8:

"For to be carnally minded is death; but to be spiritually minded is life and peace. Because the carnal mind is enmity against God: for it is not subject to the law of God, neither indeed can be. So then they that are in the flesh (carnal) *cannot please God."*

We have a serious problem – we desire to please ourselves, not God! It is difficult for us to understand the reasons why we should please God when our lives are built around who we are and what we can do. But, let's give it a start and try to understand the reasons for pleasing God instead of ourselves.

CREATION TELLS US TO PLEASE GOD!

Everything that God made was designed to bring Him pleasure. Revelation 4:11 says: *"Thou art worthy, O Lord, to receive glory and honor and power: for Thou hast created all things, and for Thy pleasure they are and were created."* That is pretty clear! He is the Creator and we are the created. All things were created to please Him. Creation by God means that we belong to Him and should fulfill His purposes for our lives. It was never His desire to see His creation honor itself. When we seek to please ourselves, we are doing what is foreign to the original design and purpose of God. It will lead to some very destructive behavior!

GOD'S SOVEREIGNTY TELLS US THAT WE SHOULD PLEASE GOD!

Man-centered theology limits God's involvement and control. It believes that God has left many things in our hands, and that He depends upon us to work things out for ourselves. We are limited by our own experiences and we rarely see things from God's point of view. Sovereignty means that God is in control!

Psalm 115:3 states it very clearly and simply: *"But our God is in the heavens: He hath done whatsoever He hath pleased."* Psalm 135:5-6 says: *"For I know that the LORD is great, and that our Lord is above all gods. Whatsoever the LORD pleased, that did He in heaven, and in earth, in the seas, and all deep places."*

WE SHOULD FOLLOW THE EXAMPLE OF YESHUA (Jesus Christ our Lord)!

If we needed a further reason to please God in all we think, say, and do, we can simple follow the example of our Lord Yeshua. He said in John 8:29: *"for I do always those things that please Him."*

Consider the argument of Romans 15:1-3 on this matter of the example of Yeshua:

"We then that are strong ought to bear the infirmities of the weak, and not to please ourselves. Let every one of us please his neighbor for his good to edification. For even Christ pleased not Himself."

OUR ACCOUNTABILITY TO GOD SHOULD MOTIVATE US TO PLEASE GOD!

The Apostle Paul wrote in II Corinthians 5:6-10 these important words:

"Therefore we are always confident, knowing that, whilst we are at home in the body, we are absent from the Lord: For we walk by faith, not by sight: We are confident, I say, and willing rather to be absent from the body, and to be present with the Lord. Wherefore we labor, that, whether present or absent, we may be accepted of Him. For we must all appear before the judgment seat of Christ; that every one may receive the things done in his body, according to that he hath done, whether it be good or bad."

Verse 9 says that whether we are still living here on earth or whether we are at home with the Lord, our goal is to be *"accepted of Him."* The word *"accepted"* is the Greek word *euarestoi* which means *"well-pleasing."* We then are told that one day we will all give account of ourselves before the *"judgment seat of Christ."*

Our accountability to God is a strong motive to do all to please Him.

THE TESTIMONY OF PAUL SHOULD ENCOURAGE US TO PLEASE GOD!

In Galatians 1:10 the Apostle Paul wrote these words: *"For do I now persuade men, or God? or do I seek to please men? for if I yet pleased men, I should not be the servant of Christ."*

Some people seem obsessed with the desire to please others and seem to ignore that motive toward God Himself.

Let's be clear about the experiences of the Apostle Paul. He suffered greatly for his commitment to the Lord. He writes about it in II Corinthians 11:23-28. But, that suffering did not move him away from his lifetime goal of pleasing God. God will sometimes bring to our lives things that are not too pleasant. Certain trials and difficulties have a way of purifying our motives regarding why we are doing what we are doing. If our reasons for what we do are not based on a strong desire to please God alone, we will not easily endure.

Paul wrote in Colossians 3:20 that children should *"obey"* their parents because *"this is well pleasing unto the Lord."* He also warned all who work for others to do it from your heart and not to do it as *"men-pleasers."*

Hebrews 13:21 says *"Make you perfect in every good work to do His will, working in you that which is well-pleasing in His sight, through Jesus Christ; to Whom be glory for ever and ever. Amen."*

SO – HOW DO WE PLEASE GOD?

No question can so revolutionize our lives as much as this one! The Bible gives us at least seven ways in which we can please God.

1. We please God by PUTTING Him first!

Matthew 3:17 speaks of how important the Son of God was and is to His heavenly Father. At His baptism by John the Baptist, a voice from heaven said: *"This is My beloved Son, in Whom I am well pleased."*

Colossians 1:15-19 is a remarkable passage dealing with the true identity of our Lord Yeshua:

"Who is the image of the invisible God, the firstborn of every creature: For by Him were all things created, that are in heaven, and that are in earth, visible and invisible, whether they be thrones, or dominions, or principalities, or powers: all things were created by Him, and for Him. And He is before all things, and by Him all things consist (hold together). And He is the head of the body, the church: Who is the beginning, the firstborn from the dead; that in all things He might have the preeminence. For it pleased the Father that in Him should all fullness dwell."

That last statement reads in the Greek text – *"all the fullness was pleased to dwell in Him."* Colossians 2:9 says: *"For in Him dwelleth all the fullness of the Godhead bodily."*

Is it not obvious that putting the Lord first in our lives and exalting our Lord Yeshua brings the Father pleasure and He is glorified as Philippians 2:9-11 clearly says: *"Wherefore God also hath highly exalted Him, and given Him a Name which is above every name: That at the Name of Jesus every knee should bow, of things in heaven, and things in earth, and things under the earth; And that every tongue should confess that Jesus Christ is Lord, to the glory of God the Father."*

To please God we must exalt His Son in our lives. A sure sign that a believer is pleasing himself is when he talks little about the Lord and much about himself!

2. We please God by PRAISING Him!

The Book of Psalms is the praise and worship book of Israel. In Psalm 69:30-31 we read: *"I will praise the Name of God with a song, and will magnify Him with thanksgiving. This also shall please the LORD better than an ox or bullock that hath horns and hoofs."*

Yes, praise is what pleases the Lord! Psalm 113:1-3 says: *"Praise ye the LORD. Praise, O ye servants of the LORD, praise the Name of the LORD. Blessed be the Name of the LORD from this time forth and for evermore. From the rising of the sun unto the going down of the same the LORD's Name is to be praised."*

Psalm 111:1 says: *"Praise ye the LORD. I will praise the LORD with my whole heart, in the assembly of the upright, and in the congregation."* Psalm 145:2 says *"I will praise Thy Name for ever and ever."*

In the New Testament, in Hebrews 13:15-16 we read the argument for praise:

"By Him therefore let us offer the sacrifice of praise to God continually, that is, the fruit of our lips giving thanks to His Name. But to do good and to communicate forget not: for with such sacrifices God is well pleased."

It is clear that we please God when we praise His Name!

3. We please God by PROCLAIMING the message of the cross!

The symbol of the cross is offensive to Jewish people because it reminds them of the persecution, torture, and murder of their ancestors by so-called Christian crusaders! But, the true impact of the cross is not that which hangs on a necklace around our necks, or that which is fixed on the architecture of a given church; the true impact is the message about what happened when our Lord Yeshua, the Jewish Messiah, died on a Roman cross almost 2000 years ago. I Corinthians 1:17-21 clearly presents the importance of the cross:

"For Christ (Messiah) *sent me not to baptize, but to preach the gospel: not with wisdom of words, lest the cross of Christ should be made of none effect. For the preaching of the cross is to them that perish foolishness; but unto us which are saved it is the power of God. For it is written* (in Isaiah 29:14), *I will destroy the wisdom of the wise, and will bring to nothing the understanding of the prudent. Where is the wise? Where is the scribe? Where is the disputer of this world? Hath not God made foolish the wisdom of this world? For after that in the wisdom of God the world by wisdom knew not God, it pleased God by the foolishness of preaching to save them that believe."*

God is pleased when the message of the gospel, the cross of our Lord Yeshua, is accurately preached under the power of the Holy Spirit! Paul wrote in Galatians

6:14: *"But God forbid that I should glory, save in the cross of our Lord Jesus Christ, by Whom the world is crucified unto me, and I unto the world."*

The cross was made out of wood. There is no efficacy in that wood. Nothing magical should be associated with it. There is no need to kiss it or worship it. The gospel is not about a piece of wood — it is about a Person Who died upon it — the Savior of the world! When we refer to the message of the cross, we are not talking about a religious symbol or an ornament to hang around one's neck. The gospel deals with what Jesus Christ did when He died on that cross. The Apostle Paul made this strong statement in I Corinthians 2:2: *"For I determined not to know any thing among you, save Jesus Christ, and Him crucified."*

That message of our Lord Yeshua, the Messiah of Israel, dying for our sins on a Roman cross over 1900 years ago — PLEASES GOD!

4. We please God by PRAYING to Him with faith!

Hebrews 11:6 says: *"But without faith it is impossible to please Him; for he that cometh to God must believe that He is, and that He is a Rewarder of them that diligently seek Him."*

So much prayer is simply talk, and little faith. Faith needs an object, and that object is God Himself. We must believe in His existence and ability to do what we ask when He wants to do it. His purposes and power are not used to make us appear to be effective in prayer! He will do what brings Him glory and praise and helps others to know Who He is and what He can do!

The writer of Hebrews says of Enoch (Hebrews 11:5): *"By faith Enoch was translated that he should not see death; and was not found, because God had translated him: for before his translation he had this testimony, that he pleased God."*

5. We please God by PURIFYING our lives!

I Thessalonians 4:1-8 is a classic passage on the importance of holiness in the life of the believer. Verse 1 says:

"Furthermore then we beseech you, brethren, and exhort you by the Lord Jesus, that as ye have received of us how ye ought to walk and to please God, so ye would abound more and more." It is clear from this opening verse that the discussion that follows is about how to please God. Please read carefully the following words from I Thessalonians 4:2-8:

"For ye know what commandments we gave you by the Lord Jesus. For this is the will of God, even your sanctification (holiness; purity), *that ye should abstain from fornication* (all kinds of sexual sin)*: That every one of you should know how to possess his vessel in sanctification and honor; Not in the lust of concupiscence, even as the Gentiles which know not God: That no man go beyond and defraud his brother in any matter: because that the Lord is the avenger of all such, as we also have forewarned you and testified. For God hath not called us unto uncleanness, but unto holiness. He therefore that despiseth, despiseth not man, but God, Who hath also given unto us His Holy Spirit."*

What pleases God? When we *"abstain from fornication."* The Greek word is *porneia* from which we get our English word "pornography." The Greek word refers to all kinds of sexual sin. Many folks speak of *"fornication"* as though it only refers to sexual intercourse before a couple gets married. That is certainly sexual sin, but the word refers to all kinds of sexual sin including adultery, incest, bestiality, homosexuality, etc.

In Ephesians 5:3-4 we read: *"But fornication, and all uncleanness, or covetousness, let it not be once named among you, as becometh saints; Neither filthiness, nor foolish talking, nor jesting, which are convenient: but rather giving of thanks. For this ye know, that no whoremonger, nor unclean person, nor covetous man, who is an idolater, hath any inheritance in the kingdom of Christ and of God."* Then, in verse 10 we read: *"Proving what is acceptable* (well-pleasing) *unto the Lord."*

We please God when we stay away from all kinds of sexual sin. Since God made us with sexual desires, what is considered pure and holy in terms of sex? Hebrews 13:4 answers: *"Marriage is honorable in all, and the bed* (coitus) *is undefiled: but whoremongers and adulterers God will judge."* Sex that is right and good (and safe!) is found within the bonds of marriage!

6. We please God by PROVIDING for the needs of others!

In Philippians 4:10-20 we have a strong example as well as an admonition to help others in time of need. The Apostle Paul illustrates this principle by using his own experience. The believers in the Roman colony of Philippi were new and needed some help in understanding. But, they had a desire to help that was unique and a blessing to Paul. Here is what he said to them:

"But I rejoiced in the Lord greatly, that now at the last your care of me hath flourished again; wherein ye were also careful, but ye lacked opportunity. Not that I speak in respect of want: for I have learned, in whatsoever state I am, therewith to be content. I know both how to be abased, and I know how to abound: every where and in all things I am instructed both to be full and to be

hungry, both to abound and to suffer need. I can do all things through Christ which strengtheneth me. Notwithstanding ye have well done, that ye did communicate with my affliction. Now ye Philippians know also, that in the beginning of the gospel, when I departed from Macedonia, no church communicated with me as concerning giving and receiving, but ye only. For even in Thessalonica ye sent once and again unto my necessity. Not because I desire a gift: but I desire fruit that may abound to your account. But I have all, and abound: I am full, having received of Epaphroditus the things which were sent from you, an odor of a sweet smell, a sacrifice acceptable, well-pleasing to God. But my God shall supply all your need according to His riches in glory by Christ Jesus. Now unto God and our Father be glory for ever and ever. Amen."

Paul makes it clear that their financial support of him in time of need was a sacrifice that truly pleased God.

Paul told the elders of the church in Ephesus in Acts 20:35: *"It is more blessed to give than to receive."*

James 3:14-17 reveals how serious this matter is of providing help to those who are in need:

"What doth it profit, my brethren, though a man say he hath faith, and have not works? Can faith save him? If a brother or sister be naked, and destitute of daily food, and one of you say unto them, Depart in peace, be ye warmed and filled; notwithstanding ye give them not those things which are needful to the body; what doth it profit? Even so faith, if it hath not works, is dead, being alone."

The faith that does not do anything is not the saving faith of the Bible! I John 3:16-18 reveals what genuine love looks like:

"Hereby perceive we the love of God, because He laid down His life for us: and we ought to lay down our lives for the brethren. But whoso hath this world's good, and seeth his brother have need, and shutteth up his bowels of compassion from him, how dwelleth the love of God in him? My little children, let us not love in word, neither in tongue; but in deed and in truth."

Once again we are confronted with the reality of our faith and love. Do we ever do anything to help others in time of need?

In addition to meeting the needs of others, our giving pleases God and causes others to give thanks to Him. God also promises to supply the needs of those who give to others.

7. We please God by <u>PRACTICING</u> obedience to Him!

I John 3:22 makes it quite clear: *"And whatsoever we ask, we receive of Him, because we keep His commandments, and do those things that are pleasing in His sight."*

According to the Bible, our sinful nature does not want to submit to authority – it rebels against it. Romans 8:7-8 states: *"Because the carnal mind is enmity against God: for it is not subject to the law of God, neither indeed can be. So then they that are in the flesh cannot please God."*

When we rebel against God's authority there is no way that we can please God.

The matter of obedience or submission to authority is a huge subject in the Bible. In the Greek New Testament there are three different words used to teach this important truth to believers who desire to please God.

1. A position of obedience

The Greek word *hupotasso* means "to arrange under" and is a military term dealing with "rank" or "position." It is used 40 times as a verb and four times as a noun in the New Testament. It is used when we are confronted with *"higher powers"* and *"rulers"* in this world (Romans 13). It is also used for the submission of wives to their husbands and children to their parents (Ephesians 5:22; I Timothy 3:4). It is the word used to instruct younger men to be careful about their response to older men (I Peter 5:5). It is used of servants (Titus 2:9) and the attitude of believers to one another (Ephesians 5:21).

2. A response of obedience

A second Greek word *hupakouo* means "to listen under" and is used 21 times as a verb and 15 times as a noun. It is used of the obedient response of children to their parents (Ephesians 6:1), and of servants to the masters (Ephesians 6:5).

3. A commitment to obedience

A third Greek word *peitharcheo* means "to persuade" and is used of Peter's remark in Acts 5:29 when he said: *"We ought to obey God rather than men."* It is used in Titus 3:1 to indicate our need to submit to political leaders and to be careful about our attitudes toward them. The direct opposite word in Greek is *apeitheo* which means "to disobey" because you are not persuaded.

That which pleases God is our submission to authority, and willingness to listen and our persuasion that this is right and good before God. James 4:7 tells us to *"Submit yourselves therefore to God."* James 4:10 adds: *"Humble yourselves in the sight of the Lord, and He shall lift you up."*

Learning to please God in all we think, say, and do fulfills God's original desire and purpose. Everything He created was made for His pleasure and glory.

The GOD of the BIBLE is personal, knowable, powerful, loving, merciful, faithful, righteous, just, gracious, kind, sovereign, longsuffering, and wants a personal relationship with us. How remarkable is that!

The GOD of the BIBLE revealed Himself in His creation, in His Word, and in the Person of His Son, our Lord Yeshua. The way to know His original purpose and plan for your life is to put your faith and trust in what His Son, our Savior, has done for you – He died for ALL of your sins, substituting Himself for the penalty that we should all pay! We deserve hell for what we have done, but His grace has provided heaven! He is NOT dead – He is alive – He arose from the dead, was seen of many people, ascended back to heaven, and has promised to come again! A fitting conclusion to your understanding of the GOD of the BIBLE would be to call upon Him right now, and trust His Son, our Savior, as your only salvation from sin, death, and hell!

GOD BLESS YOU!

BIBLIOGRAPHY

Andrews, Samuel J. *God's Revelations of Himself to Men*. New York: The Knickerbocker Press, 1901.

Bickersteth, Edward Henry. *The Trinity*. Grand Rapids: Kregel Publications, 1957.

Brown, Colin. *The New International Dictionary of New Testament Theology*, Volumes I, II, & III. Grand Rapids: Zondervan Publishing House, 1975.

Chafer, Lewis Sperry. *Systematic Theology*, Volume I. Dallas: Dallas Seminary Press, 1947.

Chapman, Colin. *Christianity on Trial*. Wheaton: Tyndale House Publishers, Inc., no date.

Chapman, Colin. *The Case for Christianity*. Grand Rapids: Wm. B. Eerdmans Publishing Co., 1981.

Charnock, Stephen. *Discourses Upon the Attributes of God*, Volumes I & II. Grand Rapids: Baker Book House, 1979.

Henry, Carl F. H. *God, Revelation, and Authority,* Volumes I-VI. Waco: Word Books, 1976.

Houston, James M. *I Believe in the Creator.* Grand Rapids: Wm. B. Eerdmans Publishing Co., 1980

Jukes, Andrew. *The Names of God in Holy Scripture.* Grand Rapids: Kregel Publications, 1967.

Kaiser, Christopher B. *The Doctrine of God.* Westchester: Crossway Books, 1982.

Knudson, Albert C. *The Doctrine of God.* New York: The Abingdon Press, 1930.

Morey, Robert. *The Trinity: Evidence & Issues.* Nashville: Nelson Bibles, 1996

Packer, J. I. *Knowing God.* Downers Grove: Inter-Varsity Press, 1972

Pink, Arthur W. *The Attributes of God.* Grand Rapids: Baker Book House, 1979.

Pink, Arthur W. *The Sovereignty of God.* London: The Banner of Truth Trust, 1972,

Rosenthal, Stanley. *One God or Three?* West Collingswood: The Spearhead Press, 1978.

Schaeffer, Francis A. *The God Who Is There.* Chicago: Inter-Varsity Press, 1968.

Shedd, William G. T. *Dogmatic Theology,* Volume I. Grand Rapids: Zondervan Publishing House, no date.

Smail, Thomas A. *The Forgotten Father.* Grand Rapids: Wm B. Eerdmans Publishing Co., 1980.

Strong, Augustus Hopkins. *Systematic Theology.* Philadelphia: the Judson Press, 1907.

Sumrall, Lester. *The Names of God.* Nashville: Thomas Nelson Publishers, 1982.

Tozer, A. W. *The Knowledge of the Holy.* New York: Harper and Row Publishers, 1961.